THE DEATH TSUNAMI

AN UNEXPECTED JOURNEY INTO
WIDOWHOOD AND HOW I MET DEATH

STEPHANIE JORDAN

CROSS OVER JORDAN

PUBLISHING
Birmingham, AL

ISBN paperback: 978-1-958441-01-5

ISBN ebook: 978-1-958441-02-2

CONTENTS

DEDICATION

I dedicate this book to my Jordan crew. We have walked through hell together and you all have made each step worth it. I couldn't have done it without you.

Jay Jordan

You. I dedicate this book to every beautiful and complex part of you. I am honored to have walked the journey of life with you. I never could have imagined the healing that came through your love and dedication to me and the Lord. You were a savior for me and my heart in many ways, and I know that you are still fighting for us in the spirit. You have left a mark and legacy here on Earth that will carry for generations. We will absolutely never forget you. Thank you for teaching me more about love than I had ever known. I will carry that with me forever. I love you!

Nautas Tidmore

Thank you for being my lighthouse in dark places. Thank you for teaching me how to grow up and giving me more to care about than myself. I want good things for you. Conquer the world with your wit, wisdom, and warrior way, Son. Jay is forever so proud of you. There wasn't a day that he didn't feel like you were his son given by God. Poppa loved you so much!

Nyah Jordan

The first born Jordan. The glue that stuck us together. Thank you for being so amazing. I appreciate the support you have given me through the years. Your dad would be so proud of you for how you lead your siblings. I see so much of Jay in you and I can't wait to see what God does with it! Poppa loved you so much!

Hammuel Jordan

You are the name bearer and the continued legacy. I am not surprised at all that God has huge things planned for your future. You have your dad's boldness and compassion. You are also a human magnet like he was. People are drawn to you, lead well. I love that you continue to bring humor and entertainment to the family. Thank you for helping guide your little sisters. They need your voice. Poppa loved you so much!

Rebekah Jordan

You exude Jay's art heart. You are so kind and funny. Thank you for being a gentle heart in a not always very kind world. Proverbs says to guard your heart, so baby girl, please make efforts to guard your tender heart. You will need to use discernment and wisdom as your life unfolds. I can't wait to see how God uses your artistic talents in your future. Poppa loved you so much!

Shiloh Jordan

Jay Jordan Jr., Jr. You are your dad made over. You have all his brilliance and complexities. You love hard like he did. I love this part about you. Thank you for being the caboose. Our family wouldn't have been complete without you. You were the gift God left all of us of Jay. He knew that the world would seem dimmer without him, so He made sure that we had his essence still here. Poppa loved you so much!

Robbie Lewis

Thank you for being a solid rock. Thank you for being there for me when I may not even fully realize it. You have always been a steady force in gale sized winds. I appreciate you. I love our history, friendships that span decades don't happen by accident. Thank you for the effort you put into loving me, even though I can be very complicated.

Tammy Wollner

All the nights that you let me pour out my brain, my hurts, my wounds, and my pain, and just listened, thank you. You may not have even realized that I needed your backbone to hold me up some nights. Being on the other side of the world actually worked well for me because that was when I had time to process some things and you were awake. It was a beautiful gift.

To my past, present, and future widows

This book is my effort to give you strength and a voice to your pain. I hope that you find clarity in this awful journey. I am honored to have walked with some of you and honored to have some of you help me through the tsunamied valley of Death. We need each other. Reach out to help those around you, and remember, keep your eyes on that pinprick of light, it is God! He will lead you out!

To everyone who helped us survive

THANK YOU!! I don't know that I can ever thank any of you enough. But THANK YOU!
We needed you! May God bless you so immensely for honoring Him and loving us.

Please use the hashtag #thedeathtsunami so I can see your posts!

Author's Note

Thank you for purchasing my book. I am grateful that you are spending your time with me as I share my journey with you. I pray that you leave encouraged, lifted up, and ready to live.

I would love to support you by having you join me on my website. I offer an online course called Believing in Boundaries to help you heal, forgive, and set healthy boundaries in your life. I have blog posts, newsletters, freebies, podcasts, and more to inspire, challenge, and encourage you. You, my reader, my fellow life traveler, are my reason to create. Thank you for being my muse!

Ebook link: The Stephanie Jordan
Browser link: https://thestephaniejordan.com/

Other titles by Stephanie:
Click or follow the links below to purchase the book in ebook or paperback form.

Believing in Boundaries:
Using Biblical Teaching to Understand and Establish Healthy Modern Boundaries

US link: https://www.amazon.com/dp/B0B1W6SQNK
UK link: https://www.amazon.co.uk/dp/B0B1W6SQNK
Canada link: https://www.amazon.ca/dp/B0B1W6SQNK

For up to date content and encouragement, follow my social media:

Instagram: https://www.instagram.com/thestephaniejordan/ @thestephaniejordan

Facebook: https://www.facebook.com/TheStephanieJordan

LinkedIn: The Stephanie Jordan

YouTube: https://www.youtube.com/@thestephaniejordan. @thestephaniejordan.

TikTok: thestephaniejordan

INTRODUCTION

I am not ready to write this book. I am not ready to venture into these emotions. I am not ready to relive all of the intensity and hard places that have been my life over the last eight years. However, I believe that God has said it is time to share my story, our story, His story. I hope that you, my reader, will find God on every single page, through every single moment. I never could have survived without His consistent guidance and faithfulness. Alas, here I am a widow, a warrior, and a survivor of the widowhood journey. I want you to feel equipped and empowered to believe (or understand) that you will also make it through the darkest days and most difficult moments of life with God. He will never leave you, nor forsake you, no matter what road you find yourself traveling.

Why do I call death a tsunami? Because Death wrecked everything in my life as far as my eye could see mentally, emotionally, physically, and spiritually. No one else can see it, no one else knows how bad the damage is, and sometimes, it seems, no one else cares. A tsunami annihilates everything in its path. It constitutes far and wide destruction and shocks even seasoned local people by how far out the water recedes into the ocean before abruptly turning around to pour much farther inland than could be expected. Death is the same way: it swoops in and creates a shockingly deep void and then it wrecks your entire existence far and wide, yet to an outsider, everything still looks completely normal on the outside. After a physical tsunami, the destruction is easily noticeable to everyone. Even though the death was personal for me, the effects were far reaching into all areas and relationships of my life. In a Death Tsunami, because it happens in the spiritual realm, much of the destruction goes unseen.

I felt like no one could see how wrecked I was. I couldn't explain it. I couldn't tell anyone how to help me because I didn't even know myself. When every single part of you is destroyed, where do you even start? Not only will death plunge you straight into the Valley of the Shadow of Death, but it will blind you with how dark it is. In Psalms 23, it is written, "Though I walk through the Valley of the Shadow of Death." The Bible refers to facing the aftermath of death as the shadow of death. The shadow. The tsunami of death is all the destruction that happens in the aftermath of Death coming. The shadow is the darkness that prevents you from being able to see, and the vulnerability that comes after death. Think of Death like a huge tsunami wave that can move across the Earth. The height, depth, and width are unimaginable in size because it is a spiritual principle. When it comes and takes a human life, the wave passes and that is the tsunami wreckage. The shadow of darkness comes, similar to a storm in the middle of the night, and covers like a dense fog that is impossible to see through. Daylight never comes, maybe even for years. There is no light in a shadow. That is why it is a shadow. There is no light in that valley, and it is so dark that you can't see your hand in front of your face. There was a small pin prick of light, the tiniest spot. I locked my eyes on it, for I knew that is where God was. I knew that if I focused on that light, it would shine a light unto my path, and my feet and I would make it out alive. Not only would I make it, but I could lead my kids out too, if they willingly follow. God is there, much like a spotlight, illuminating each step to get you back into the light.

Have you ever seen *The Never Ending Story*? I love that movie so much. There is a character in the movie called The Great Nothing. That is a great representation of death. The Great Nothing left nothing in its wake and it had no care for what it destroyed. The difference between this movie character and real life is that the character was seen coming. Death is never seen coming. Even if it is known that someone is dying, there is not any way to know exactly when their last moment is. One minute there is life, then the next, the Great Nothing has come, and there is utter destruction behind it with a shadow so dark that one can't see.

Chapter 1

OUR STORY

In August 2003, I was at a music show with my son.
We were out front standing on the sidewalk talking to a
friend. Here comes this beat up truck, rickety and speed-
ing around the corner, and my friend says, "Hey! There's
Pineapple Butt." I turned to look, but it didn't really
mean anything to me. Pineapple Butt had never really
liked me since we were teens. I was the only Christian
in the Birmingham punk rock scene, and he had always
hated me because of it. I never tried to get to know him,
and he avoided me, so it was kind of a mutually respected
distance. I was always sober as a teen. I never was interested in drugs, alcohol, and debauchery. I was a Christian, though I was broken. Pineapple Butt's goal was to
die at twenty-one in New Orleans on a drug overdose.
He hated me because of my faith. He hated God, hated
Jesus, hated anything Christians represented. He was so
against the idea of Christianity that if he could do anything against it, he would. Anything. Everything. His an-
them was to destroy.

However, in his early twenties, he met God on God's terms. He was introduced to the love of Jesus through a family that meant the world to him. Instead of overdosing on his twenty-first birthday, Jay Jordan was baptized in New Orleans. Instead of dying to life, he was born again. An opportunity to live life to the full. He said becoming a Christian was the worst thing and best thing that ever happened to him. He had to recognize that all the awful things he had done, prior to knowing Christ, were sins. There was a plethora of sin to sort through. He also appreciated that Jesus took it all to the cross and didn't make him pay for it. He indeed embraced life, especially the one that God had in store for him. We met a few years after this pivotal event. Although we knew of each other, and had been in the same places at the same time, we hadn't actually ever spoken, until the God ordained day.

He walked up wearing a huge T-shirt, baggie jeans cut off at the ankles, and Birkenstocks. Ew! What a mess he was! He sauntered over to where we were and just chimed in like he had been included the entire time. "Hi. I'm Jay. Or Pineapple Butt, you can call me either." It is common in the punk rock and biker scene to have nicknames. Pineapple Butt was originally given to Jay at about thirteen years old to hurt his feelings. But in these scenes, you either have tough skin and embrace what people try to break you with, or you will never make it. Jay embraced Pineapple Butt and was endearly known as that for most of his life and by pretty much everyone he knew.

Pineapple Butt, it turned out, was friendly, even funny. I didn't think much about it because I knew he didn't like me. But, surprisingly, he told me that he had become a Christian. I rolled my eyes. Ooooof course he had! (Really, I thought he was just hitting on me at this point.)

We talked about how cool it would be to have a ministry geared towards punk rock kids and those who were struggling, like drug addicts and prostitutes. He asked me for my phone number and stretched out his shirt. Um. In my mind, I was thinking, "No big deal, Stephanie. You can throw it off by a number, and it'll be fine. He won't find me." So, I grabbed the pen and started writing my phone number directly on his T-shirt. But when I got to the last number, I paused. I hesitated, ready to throw in a big fat ol' lie that would keep him from calling me. Then I wrote it. I wrote the 9. What? Wait! Did I just do that? Did I actually write down my legit phone number?! Well. Crap. He now had my phone number.

It was almost like God wouldn't allow me to give him the wrong number. Had this human disaster known as Pineapple Butt just stepped into my life as a God-ordained, God-appointed person?

The next day, about 7:00 p.m., he called me on my cell phone.

"Hello?"

"Hi, this is Jay. We met yesterday."

"Yes, Jay. I know exactly who you are."

And four hours later, we said goodnight. Of course I reminded him that my phone plan wasn't free until after 9:00 p.m., so he would need to wait to call me until then.

Every night at nine, Jay called me like clockwork. Because of my experience with domestic violence in my previous marriage, I wouldn't let Jay come to my house. I was living alone with my son, and I wasn't about to take the chance that this huge man would be alone with us. Jay was patient, though he begged me to give him a chance to prove that he was safe. It took nearly a month before I let him come over. We geared up our conversation about starting a ministry together. R.I.O.T. (Reaching Into Our Territory) was about to be born in Birmingham, Alabama. Our focus was to reach punk rockers, hardcore kids, skateboarders, drug addicts, prostitutes, and really anyone who was used to walking off the beaten path and to the beat of their own drum and needed to be accepted.

This ministry sparked a friendship between Jay and me. We started spending a lot of time together. One night, he was at my house sitting in my recliner. I was on my couch. Now, maybe I should share a little bit about myself. I am extremely blunt. I am not shy. I am not afraid of confrontation or making things a little uncomfortable. Jay could've used that information up front, and it might have helped him through this conversation. So, we are in my den. My son had gone to bed, and we were just hanging out.

I said, "Jay, can we get over this little awkward thing and just be friends? It's never going to happen. I am not going to date you, so can we just move on so it isn't weird?"

He said, "I've never been so uncomfortable in my life. I mean, I guess so."

There it was. Called out into the wide open. I had just dropped the bomb and shattered his hopes of us dating. I figured it would help us to not have a big elephant in the room every time we were together. It didn't really sway Jay at all. He just continued right on dating me, without my consent, for months. Our ministry caused us to spend a lot of time together. We were living life out with our group and each other. We were very involved in many churches around our area.

One extremely cold night, Jay rode a Ninja 250 from his home to mine. It was an hour one way, and when he showed up, his eyelids were basically frozen to his eyeballs, and he had icicles on his lashes. He was nearly frost bitten, and was a gigantic ice cube. I could not believe that he rode a motorcycle in that weather, but wherever I was, is where he intended to be. I guess his big huge heart full of the fire of love kept him warm enough to endure the ride.

In November 2003, we took a trip to Texas for a conference. Our R.I.O.T. crew piled in a friend's Ford Expedition, and we spent the weekend at this conference. We all hated the conference, so we left it early and just enjoyed the trip. We ate at fun restaurants and went to the mall. He let me shop while he watched my young son. He always acted like my son was already his own. It was a pivotal weekend for us. We became best friends on this trip. We created so many inside jokes, I probably laughed more than I had ever in my life. There it was, the key to my heart, laughter. Laughter was never in short supply with Jay. He was hilarious. However, I still had no intention of dating him!

December came and for my birthday, he gave me an incredibly cool piece of art that he had made for my gift. I was flattered that he had spent so many hours working on this piece of art. It was a huge canvas with a graphite on black paint image of Jesus' eyes and crown of thorns. It fit so beautifully over my fireplace. He tortured himself with some chick flick and mediocre Mexican food. It was still an amazing night to him, because he was with me.

Jay helped me move from one house to another in January 2004. That night, after everyone left, Jay was sitting in a chair across the room, and he said, "I love you."

I said, "I know."

He exclaimed, "YOU KNOW?!"

I said, "Of course I do. You have shown me that you love me for months."

He was a bit speechless. But I did know. Jay was always there for me. He was an encourager and my biggest fan. If there was ever a way to say "I love you" without words, Jay Jordan had mastered it.

In February 2004, Jay and I had our first date. Fort Payne, Alabama, used to be called the "Sock Capital of the World" because it had so many sock factories. We did a lot of homeless ministry with R.I.O.T., and we were gathering socks for our next outing. We ended up at a nice restaurant in the mountains of northern Alabama on Valentine's Day. It was romantic. Over the months of our friendship, Jay had really proven himself. He was a constant, and he made things happen that needed to happen. He loved my son like he was his own. He told me that my mothering was one of the reasons he fell in love with me. According to Jay, he had had a terrible upbringing and a childhood saturated with neglect and abuse. He loved that I was an engaged mother. I was flattered by how much he noticed and complimented it.

One day, Jay was asleep on the couch. My son had woken up earlier than us, and he walked up to Jay—mind you he was two years old—and said,"Eggonme."

Jay said, "Comere, little buddy," and proceeded to attempt to pick him up. Then the light bulb went off. OH! Egg. On. Me. So Jay came upstairs and woke me up in my room and said,"Uuuuhhh, I think you might want to wake up. There's something downstairs that you need to see."

I got up and walked downstairs and wowza!! What a mess! There was baby powder and baby shampoo all over the living room and then the eggs... The "egg on me" eggs were everywhere. Seventeen out of eighteen eggs were broken all over the kitchen and living room. We called the one survivor, Nemo. Now, what you need to know about Jay for this story to be relevant is that he hated, loathed, and despised snot or viscous texture of any kind. It absolutely grossed him out and made him ill. So the fact that he was on his hands and knees, practically gagging, close to vomiting, to clean up the nearly dozen broken raw eggs off the covered kitchen floor, was further proof that he indeed loved me very much.

One weekend in May 2004, we were at a conference at the church I grew up in, and I heard God tell me that my new name would be Jordan. I was like, nope! God, I'll take any man on the planet but Jay Jordan! I had prayed against him no less than a thousand times at this point. I mean, that man was a hot mess! No steady income. No home of his own. No driver's license! He didn't have anything pulled together. There was no way, absolutely no way under the sun that I was going to marry this man! Dating him was one thing, but marrying him was something else entirely. How did God expect me to marry a man with no driver's license?

I set an appointment with the pastor at the church. He told me that the Jordan River is a prominent place in the Bible, so I needed to study a bit about the Jordan. I did. The Jordan River is God's dwelling place. Ugh. *"Does that mean I have to marry this guy??"* was my thought process.

So, I prayed for three signs in hopes that I wouldn't have to go through with it. I asked for one sign to be from someone I trusted; a second sign from a really random but obvious place; and a third sign from God's word, the Bible. I got all three signs answered. The first sign was from my mom over lunch one day. She shared her story about how she knew God called her into her marriage with my stepdad. She just knew that she was supposed to marry him.

The second sign was given when Pepa, from Salt-N-Pepa (look them up if you don't know who they are because you should! They were fundamental in my early years of life. Maybe not the greatest influence for a young girl, but I still love their beats!), shared her story on a Christian TV show that I never watched until I was flipping through and saw her on it. And there was sign two. I stopped and watched her share that no matter what you have gone through, God can redeem it. No matter what you have done, God can redeem it. If you come from a broken marriage, God can redeem it. Sign two was that God was going to redeem my brokenness from being divorced by calling me into a marriage He ordained.

After the pastor mentioned that the Jordan River is a prominent place in the Bible, I sat down and wrote out all the scripture references that mentioned the river. I began to write the scriptures out so that I would be able to focus on what was being said about the river. The final sign came from the story in 2 Kings 5:1-14 in which Elisha told the king, who was a leper, to go bathe in the Jordan seven times and he would be renewed like a young boy. There it was, the third sign from God's Word, just as I had asked. Although this passage completed the third sign, the full significance of this scripture wouldn't be revealed until much later in my life's journey.

OK, God. I hear you. I will marry this Jordan man. But first he had to get his driver's license. Jay's license was suspended for failure to appear in court from a DWI charge he had had many years before I met him. We drove to the municipality, and he turned himself in. He gave me the money to bail him out. After I bailed him out, I went home, and he went to court the next day. The judge gave him time served and a fine, which he paid. Then he was able to get his driver's license, moving him one step closer to being marriage material.

Our Wedding
and Building a Family

I told Jay on a Sunday that I would marry him. He called Sloss Furnaces National Historic Museum to see if we could get married there. They were stunned, no one had ever asked to be married there before. They agreed and asked us to donate $50 to the museum. We chose a black and white theme, which was really cool in contrast with the rusty, deep iron red background. Three days later, on a Wednesday, June 30, 2004, I became a Jordan, with my little son as our ring bearer. I began my descent into the "Jordan River" to be eventually renewed, after I first became destroyed by the death tsunami. I know that sounds backwards, maybe. In retrospect, I had no idea how backwards it would feel to experience it. I expected my promised renewal to come in the form of a happy marriage. Instead it came after one of the hardest, darkest places I have ever been. However, I learned that this journey would be probably one of the most important journeys of my life. Sometimes I lament the struggle, but I am forever grateful for the love and compassion and faithfulness that God has shown me through every single step.

We got pregnant three weeks after we got married with our first daughter. God knew we were going to need more than a sheet of paper to keep this family together. Jay was ecstatic. Me, not so much. I was excited about the baby but terrified about being pregnant because of the nightmare situation that I had with my first pregnancy and domestic violence. I didn't realize how that situation would cause me to withdraw from Jay. That challenge led Jay to entertain the idea of using drugs again. He had been sober for quite a while, but a guy he was working with had started bringing drugs around. Jay wasn't strong enough to resist, and eventually he gave in, which threw our marriage into a full tailspin. We were in total chaos with a baby on the way.

The finale of his drug use came just before he went into rehab in November 2006, but there was a lot of damage that was done in our marriage. A year-long battle with his addictions and having two young kids, while I was also building my business, was a very difficult season in our lives. There were many days that I hated him because I felt like I was carrying the weight of our marriage alone. We were unhappy many times in our marriage because I struggled to forgive him, and he struggled to know how to repair the hurts. There was chaos, and there were some really beautiful moments. I am sure that most relationships experience some of that same pendulum swing, ours just seemed to have a lot of force behind each swing that carried us to extremes.

I got pregnant with our third child while he was in rehab. Bad timing, I know. But it was God's timing. God had told me that Jay wouldn't finish the full program, but had He told me it was because I was going to get pregnant, I most likely would've tried to prevent that, which is exactly why He didn't tell me. My control issues would have intervened on God's plan. The day I took my pregnancy test, Jay called me and told me that he thought God told him it was time to come home. Jay and

I weren't able to talk during the week, so I was surprised by the phone call. I asked him what his counselor said, and Jay replied,"He thinks I have heard from God."

I answered, "Well, that's good because I took a pregnancy test today, and I am pregnant."

He said,"Well, that is just confirmation for me."

I went and picked him up from rehab. I got about five minutes down the road and slammed on the breaks in the middle of the road. I turned and looked at Jay and asked, "Am I taking home a husband or a problem?"

He answered, "A husband."

My son was prophesied. I had told Jay and my mentor a few weeks prior that I felt like God was telling me that we would have a son and to name him Hammuel. They asked me if I was pregnant, and I told them no. I mean, certainly God wouldn't have given me another child while my husband was in rehab! I was surprised at the timing, but not that he was coming. In November 2007, a full year after Jay's surrender to get sober and stay sober, we had our son. He was a bright light in a dark time. I was still very unsure that we would make it through the repairing of our marriage. I believe that we fought so hard because we had these small people that needed us. They gave us motivation to keep going and keep pulling together, even in the times we felt so far apart on our inside.

Over the next few years, we were busy growing family life. I was diligently working on building my business. He was a stay-at-home dad. Originally that was our plan when the economy tanked in 2008, but after we bought our house in 2010, he was supposed to go back to work at our metal company, Exodus Iron and Forge. We ended up dissolving the company, and Jay never went back to a formal job. A year after we moved into our home, Jay caught the kitchen on fire, so we were without a kitchen for nearly a year as we rebuilt it. This nightmare made me realize that we could never build a house together. It wasn't a difference in taste that was the issue, but a difference in understanding how critical a kitchen is for a family of five people. He didn't seem to have the same need to have a working one. We had plenty of dramatic fights that led to more space between our hearts.

Jay lost his mom, who was sick for many years. Then his sister-in-law passed away with cancer. These were both devastating losses for him. In my ignorance, I didn't have very much compassion for his grieving. Everyday was so full and so busy, there was no time for grief. A foolishness on my part for sure. We had moved across town from my work, so I was gone a bit more and for longer hours. It was harder to fit in all the daily tasks, and frustrations ran high regularly. Jay struggled with depression and would have high highs and low lows. Though he was never fully diagnosed, he and I both thought that he suffered from bipolar disorder, which explained much of his self medicating tendencies. He struggled with erratic behaviors, and sometimes he would sleep for three days at a time. These shut downs were usually after a manic episode of hyper focus for two to three days. The roller coaster was an exhausting ride.

In July 2011, Jay had me arrested for domestic violence. The irony is that it was exactly ten years after I had been abused by my ex-husband. Did I hit him? Yes. Why? This is a complicated story, but it really boils down to the fact that I did not handle a situation well. However, I went to jail for what he did to himself, not what I had done. He hit himself over and over again in the face because he was full of drama and anger—and then called the police on me. It was a trump move and I paid for it. He tried to bail me out, but they wouldn't let him. I sat in jail for twelve hours and read Frances Chan's *Crazy Love*. God told me to forgive him that night. I said, "Absolutely no way in heck am I forgiving him for this!! Do you know what all I have put up with from him!?" The next morning at 7:00 a.m., my mother picked me up from the city jail. I went to file for legal separation that day. I was ready for this nightmare marriage to be over and done with for good. But God.

Forgiveness was the consistent theme that we were called to over and over again. God consistently drew us back together after every single dip we managed to hit, and there were a lot of them. We had many reasons to fight for each other, but often we fought with each other.

Jay had a way of being very demonstrative. Every movement and everything he did was big. Larger than life. He loved big. His anger was big. His heart was the biggest. It was hard to stay mad at him sometimes because of his beautiful heart and regal spirit. I couldn't have grown with anyone else the way I did with Jay. God had ordained it, and it was a breathtaking journey. We were sealed together as one flesh, and we had so much fruit to show for it.

Life was full. Each year of our marriage had huge events. I always say that this is when the Rockies were built in the panoramic view of my life. If I look at my life like a panoramic picture, there are valleys, hills, mountains, rivers, and oceans. It is a full-spectrum view of a fully lived life. There were really low moments for us as we battled through Jay's addiction issues and super high moments as we had beautiful babies.

Chapter 2

2014

I will actually start this chapter in 2012. I am not sure that I can explain the complexity of 2014 without building up the importance of the two years prior. In January 2012, I opened my hair salon storefront called Beauty for Ashes Salon and Colorbar. I had had two prophecies prior to opening: 1) I would have the salon for seven years, 2) My daughter would be born one year after we moved into our space.

We moved into the space on New Years Eve, 2011 and officially started business on January 3, 2012. In April, 2012, I got pregnant with Rebekah. I know the exact days I got pregnant because God told me to have sex with Jay. I told Jay that we had just gotten pregnant with Rebekah, and he told me that I ruin everything by knowing everything. I knew when she would be born, what her name was, and when we got pregnant. But I certainly didn't know everything! There was so much coming ahead that took me by total surprise!

In November 2012, at thirty-seven weeks pregnant, my back went out, and I could not stand up. I was rushed to the emergency room and spent the next few days in the hospital trying to figure out what was going on with my back. An orthopedic doctor saw me and ordered an MRI (non-magnetic since I was so pregnant), and they realized that my L5-S1 disc was in extremely bad shape. They gave me an epidural block so that I could get back on my feet. I had to be on a walker for the rest of my pregnancy because if I fell, I might have been paralyzed for the rest of my life. Pregnancy causes instability since it changes the center of gravity. It was a sight to see me on that walker.

I got out of the hospital on Tuesday, my grandmother died on Wednesday, and Thursday was Thanksgiving. My brother told me on Sunday at the funeral that I looked the most pathetic he had ever seen me—like I had aged sixty years overnight! The next month was quite challenging. Rebekah was born on New Years Eve, 2012, exactly one year after we moved into our space.

In April, 2013, my epidural block wore off, and I couldn't stand up again. I went to a chiropractor, and he told me that I was in really bad shape. Rather than adjust me, he sent me to see a neurosurgeon, and on May 9, 2013, I had to have emergency back surgery. It absolutely traumatized me. I couldn't pick up my baby. I had to quit taking all pain meds three days after my surgery because it dried up my breast milk, and I wasn't willing to give that up because of the importance of it for my baby. Jay would bring her to me and twenty minutes later would flip her to the other side. I literally could not pick my baby up for many months. That was devastating as well. I went back to work ten days after my surgery. I had a business to run, and I was so scared that I wasn't going to make it if I wasn't there to make money for the salon. A sweet client prayed over me for healing in my back in

October, 2013. After this prayer was the first time I was able to pick my baby up myself since my back surgery.

By the end of 2013, Jay and I had decided that we would get divorced after the New Year. We were over it, over each other, over the hurdles, over life. We were done with each other. It was kind of a relief. We survived our way into 2014, barely speaking.

Early January, probably the first week, Jay was putting up cameras in the salon. I was knitting by the fire at home. I felt a "bump, bump, bump, bump," in my tummy. I thought to myself, "Either that was some heck of some muscle memory, or that was a baby!!" I called Jay and told him that I thought I just felt a baby move. He asked me if I was trying to freak him out, and I told him to go ahead because I was freaking out. See, God had such a fantastic sense of humor that we did not laugh at, at all. Since He knew that Jay and I would be such a disaster, He gave us people. Lots of people to keep this crazy train together! And here was another Jordan baby on the way.

Now, you may wonder, like Jay, how in the world did I not know that I was pregnant with my fifth child?! Well, I was so broken. I had just had a baby and back surgery, and in October, we had decided to get divorced. It truly never crossed my mind, and she never moved... until that day she did. God told me, *She is a treasure.* He had hidden her until it was time (right about the time we had decided to get divorced) to reveal her. Good play, God. TKO! So, Jay and I waved our white flag of defeat and limped and struggled through the majority of 2014. You can picture us both like Wile E. Coyote from the Road Runner cartoons. That is exactly how we felt by the Spring of 2014. We were drained of any ability to fight. Fight God. Fight each other. Fight life.

Jay and I had four children together, and he was always the father to my oldest son, though he was not his biologically. We were raising five children together. Life was full and complex. That summer, Jay started praying every single night that God would heal the broken little girl inside of me. I didn't understand the prayer. At least not then, but I would come to an understanding of the power of it.

At the beginning of October, 2014, we went to a conference at the church that was led by the man who introduced Jesus to Jay. I wouldn't let Jay even hold my hand, much less desired any other kind of affection from him. Thankfully, they had child care and we were able to take our two little girls ("the littles") with us. On the very first night, the Holy Spirit got ahold of me and changed everything. As I lay on the floor, filled with a dense Holy Spirit presence, I asked, "Teach me to be a good wife." The Saturday lunch session offered us the opportunity to get outside and enjoy the beautiful Southern day with its warm, crisp air and cool breeze. A sure sign that fall is near. I was standing on the corner of the park, looking toward a small row of stores when I heard it. The Holy Spirit speaking to my core. "If you leave him, you will always long for him." But it didn't end with just the words. I felt it in my gut. A longing, a devastation, an utter regret, an emptiness. The message was brief. This feeling lasted maybe seconds in time but imprinted itself on my heart, mind, and soul. We finished the conference and went home.

October 11th was Jay's thirty-eighth birthday. He went to a local motorcycle event that is held annually.

On October ninth, the Holy Spirit said, "Go offer yourself to your husband."

I said, "Nope! Do you see this bed full of babies???!! It is midnight! I am not going to offer myself to him!"

Again, "Go offer yourself to your husband, and do not leave him vulnerable."

Ugh. Ugh. I got up. Reluctant at first. I didn't even want Jay to touch me for months. I walked outside and kissed his ear. He said, "Why are you being so nice to me?" (I still laugh in my mind, even as I write this because there wasn't a single piece of me that wanted to be nice to him. But telling your husband it is obedience to God isn't exactly foreplay.) I didn't answer, but I offered myself to my husband, and it was beautiful. The Holy Spirit penetrating every moment with healing. In case you're wondering, NO, I did not get pregnant!

The next day I went to work. It was a Friday, the day he would be leaving for this motorcycle event and the day before his birthday. My cell phone rang, but I didn't hear it. Then the salon phone rang, and my manager said, "Jay is looking for you desperately." I called him back when I got a chance.

He was super breathy. "I didn't know she was coming! I made her leave the moment she got here!"

I said, "Who?"

He answered. And unfortunately, I can't tell you all of this and not tell you how we got to this moment. Jay had an ex-girlfriend that liked to "borrow" my husband. Originally, I was OK with the relationship and didn't feel threatened by it at all. Somewhere along the way, things changed, and she was encroaching on my territory. I told him that he couldn't hang out with her unless I was around. I had a little birdie tell me that he had seen them at a Chick-Fil-A one day at lunch with our kids. This was during the time we had a lot of distance in our relationship, and it was very shady. I told him that he wasn't allowed to see her anymore at all. I never worried about him cheating on me. I told you that he dated me for months before I ever paid him any attention. If there was one thing on this planet that I knew, it was that Jay Jordan loved me and me alone. However, I knew that she had every intention of digging her claws in if the opportunity arose. I believe that is what she came to try to do that day. The day after my obedience to the Lord left no room for someone other than me to be on Jay's mind! God knew. God knew that she was going to show up the next day. God knew her heart. God knew her intentions. God knew and protected us. Protected Jay. Protected the Jordan line.

Jay went to his event that weekend, and when he came home, we had fast food for dinner. He was exhausted and left his wrappers on the table. The next morning we got up and went to church. As I was walking out of the house, I passed by the wrappers and rolled my eyes, and there it was again. The voice. "Don't say anything. Keep your mouth shut. Just throw it away and move on." Insert eyeroll here. But I did as I was told and threw the paper away and moved on without a word.

We rolled through November with miraculous healing continuing to happen in our marriage. On December 12, 2014, I was coming home from a long day at work and an event with the kids and he called me. "When are you coming home?"

"Why?"

"I miss you!"

"You do?? You MISS me?"

He hadn't said words like that in years. He probably hadn't actually missed me in years but was relieved when I was gone. Things in our marriage weren't easy.

He said, "Yes. I miss you. I am enjoying you more than I have in years."

I asked, "Do you want to know why?"

"Sure."

I told him how the Holy Spirit had been walking me through each day. Telling me when to shut my mouth and when to forgive and when to overlook things I wanted to be angry about. I had been kinder and more graceful as the Holy Spirit was leading me everyday.

"I can totally see that," he said.

December 24th is our family's special day. I was sick and had a low-grade fever. We went about the evening participating in our family traditions. Christmas morning, I was still sick and by then Jay was sick. I went to my mom's house early because I needed help with my kids. I needed sleep and Jay was out of it and couldn't help me. December 28th was the first day that he got out of bed. He was feeling much better but was still weak.

December 29th I went to work to change the POS system at the salon. I spent the majority of the day there. It was a Monday. I got home that evening around 5:00 p.m. We ate dinner and later we started to put the kids to bed. Jay did that task most of the time. He was complaining about his arm hurting. He got in the shower, which was always his way of soothing himself. I was on the phone with a friend and doing deposits for the next day. He was getting louder and louder. Jay could be very dramatic, so this did not set off an alarm to me. I was used to his boisterous and loud exclamations. I was desensitized to his drama. He came and lay on our bed and asked me to rub his back, thinking he was having gas bubbles.

I stood up off my side of the bed and walked the three steps to the end of the bed. He flopped over and started seizing. I asked him if he was messing with me. I grabbed my phone and looked in his eyes and saw his pupil blow out... then he went blue. I started to scream for someone to help me! I called 911. I sent my kids across the street because I had woken them screaming. The babies slept in bed. I tried to do CPR. He never told me to call for help. He never alerted me to call 911. He never gave me the heads up that I needed to get help. I was thirty-seven. He was thirty-eight! Who thinks that someone is about to die of hypertension? I knew nothing about heart issues! There he was. Dead.

The ambulance came, and I left the room. They called it at 12:03 a.m. on December 30, 2014. This date was a lie, of course, because this had all happened on December 29th. Those three minutes were liars. Those three minutes didn't count to my head, heart, or death.

Jay Jordan was dead.

I had just watched my husband of ten and a half years die. Like, he just died. Right then and there. The spiritual tsunami of Death had entered our home and wrecked every single thing. Nothing was untouched. I wanted to vomit. I tried so hard not to vomit. Where did my breath go? My breath was stolen. I wanted to vomit. I couldn't breathe. Time stopped.

I sat with my dead husband on my bedroom floor until the coroner came to take him away. I was there the moment the last breath of air left his lungs. It was a surreal moment to watch this man, who was always larger than life, leave it. One of the devastations of losing ten and a half years of marriage is that I felt we had just crested the infancy stage of marriage. We had just come to accept each other for who we are. We knew who the other one was and what would and would not change, we had healed through some hard stuff, and made it to a place of acceptance. Not just tolerance, but actual appreciation. Now it was gone. In a blink. Poof.

Chapter 3

THE FOG

Everyone showed up. My parents. My best friend. Jay's dad. People. I went to gather my kids from the neighbors' house. They were begging to know what was going on. It was 3:00 a.m. Jay was then gone. I sat with my tender seven-year-old son in my lap. I couldn't breathe. I tried so hard not to vomit.

I think I went to bed, but it seemed like it was dawn by then. I lay in bed and cried. People were starting to hear the news. I had no energy. I couldn't breathe. The dense fog of death rolled in over me. I was no longer present in my heart, mind, or soul. Sometime the next day, I walked into my dining area. I sat. It seemed like I was there for hours. Fog. So much fog. I couldn't breathe.

My sweet "sisters," mostly my homeschool mom friends, and my bestie were tending to my kids, my house, me. I think I ate. Fog. The next day was Rebekah's (baby number four) second birthday. They threw her a party. It was so sweet. She deserved to be celebrated. I couldn't breathe.

You know in the movies when someone is sitting or standing and the world is spinning around them a million miles an hour, and they are still? That was me. The world seemed to keep moving, and I was standing still. I was in some kind of time warp from hell that had stolen my breath. I don't know who was here. Who was doing what. Just fog. So. Much. Fog.

My brain had gone into some kind of hibernation mode. It was like it had shut off on me involuntarily. Trying to search and make sense of it all, but left wanting seemed to be my perpetual state of being.

My brother came into town at some point and took me and the kids to visit a friend's cotton farm in northern Alabama. I thought it would be good for the kids to get away for a couple of days, and I thought maybe I could breathe again. That night on the farm, I believe it was about five days after Jay passed away, I went to sleep, and in my dream I told someone that Jay had passed away. I awoke with a jolt and began to sob. I went to the bathroom hoping not to disturb anyone. Uncontrollable, guttural, knee-bending sobbing on the bathroom floor; all my heart poured out of my eyes. I have no idea how long I was there on that floor, but it was the moment that my heart, head, and soul finally registered that Jay Jordan had died, and it nearly killed me. If sobbing could kill someone, I would've died on the bathroom floor of a stranger's farmhouse that night. I couldn't breathe. So much fog.

The memorial service was the following Sunday. It was beautiful. There were prophetic evangelists, a pagan priest, Christian bikers, non-Christian bikers, drug addicts straight out of prison, your average suburban grandma, and everything in between. It spoke so beautifully to how Jay lived and loved. How he never forgot where he came from but allowed Jesus to do the incredible redeeming work and change him into an entirely different man. It honored Jay; it honored God. The same pastor who did the church conference in October, Greg, did Jay's memorial service in January. He shared funny stories because Jay was hilarious. He shared hard times because Jay had had plenty of those. The kids and I got up on the stage so everyone could see his incredible legacy, and we could take in all the love these people were sharing with us for Jay. It was an incredible gift and Jay would've loved every second of it.

When I went home from that, I felt like I had been hit by a train. I couldn't breathe.

The day after his memorial service, my ex-husband and his girlfriend were staying at my house to help me. Weird, I know. He and Jay were friends too. The ex and I had had a peaceful divorce over the years. I walked into the den, and they both said, "Whoa! You look like shit!"

I said, "I feel like shit!"

They offered to let me go back to bed and guaranteed they would take care of my kids. I took them up on the offer, and I don't remember when I resurfaced. I couldn't breathe. So much fog.

After about ten days, I had to get back to work. The daycare was absolutely amazing and loved us by allowing both my little girls to attend immediately. Rebekah was attending the daycare, but Shiloh wasn't. The daycare made sure to make room for Shiloh. They were devastated to hear the news. I went back to work. It is all fog.

I do remember someone coming by and telling me they were interested in shooting a commercial in my salon. I don't even remember answering them but just watching them walk away almost surreal in slow motion. I was in a time warp. I couldn't form full thoughts or sentences. My body ached. My heart ached. I wasn't married, but I was married in my heart, in my soul. I felt like I had been run over or in a fist fight that I had lost. Every joint was sore. I cried all the time. Shampooing my clients with tears streaming down my face was common.

The fog lasted for months. Nothing was normal. There was no such thing as "new normal." That stale term is supposed to bring some kind of comfort or encouragement to a broken heart. For me, it felt like a punch in the gut.

Normal. I hate that word. Nothing is normal. Nothing will ever be normal after the spiritual tsunami of death overruns it. Why can't I breathe?

Chapter 4

THE FIVE KIDS

My sweet kids. All five of them were impacted in such deep and different ways. Jay and I always tried to instill strong family bonds, and I saw that blossom in the trials that lay ahead for us. I saw my nine-year-old daughter and seven-year-old son pull together and support each other. It was pretty amazing to see.

There is, of course, no manual on how to handle children and grief. There is no easy way to navigate waters you feel like you are drowning in, much less have five little people who need so much of you. I can see a million graces of God in every step that we stayed alive in those years. For years I lived with the concept of, "If we are alive at the end of today, we have won." It was truly survival in many primal ways.

I was breastfeeding my youngest the same day that Jay passed, the next day, I wasn't breastfeeding anymore. If you haven't ever breastfed, or been exposed to the process of it, there is usually a slow but sure weaning period. Sometimes children get just one feeding a day for a longer period of time, but not this time. Like death, it just stopped. That may sound like a simple thing, but it was a mark. Another mark of how things were immediately changed. I had to find babysitters immediately because Jay stayed at home with the kids. It isn't easy to find people who are willing to stay with five children. It isn't easy to find people who will invest in your children well. I had babysitters that robbed us. They stole everything that they possibly could. I was vulnerable, and the wolves are always out. We homeschooled, so finding someone who was willing to do that was even more of a challenge.

Of course, I had to pay them. I didn't get a single penny of social security for any of my children. They told me it had been too long since Jay had paid in. It didn't matter that his social security number was on every single quarterly and yearly return I had made for ten years. Nope. That didn't count. I was on my own.

God, in His majesty, made it all work. It all worked, and we all survived those years. The first three to four were the most challenging. I struggled to think. My brain went into a hibernation-like mode, and the fact that I survived, much less all five of my kids, is a testimony to the faithfulness of God. There is absolutely no way I can take credit for our survival. Yes, I got up. Yes, I managed to take care of all the things. Yes, I was an active part in our survival, but I am not the one who kept us alive and moving forward. That was God.

I don't know that I even have enough memories to go into details about everything that happened with my kids. But it seemed like the death was just the initial challenge that we would face; the uphill climb in the dark began very quickly afterwards. My youngest had been fighting a cold for two weeks, and we had the hardest time getting her well. She was a bit miserable.. Thankfully, we started going to a chiropractor at that time, and that helped resolve her cold.

Two months after the Death Tsunami came, my oldest son had to have emergency surgery. That situation was terrifying for me because my kids had always been so healthy. I was so afraid something would happen to him. Then the youngest spent a few days in the hospital about two weeks after his surgery because she had croup. We all had physical issues and ailments that next year, our bodies grieving along with our hearts.

Each child struggled through their own journey of sorrow, lack of support, stepping up and living through the hardest loss they have ever had up until this point. I don't think I knew much of what they went through individually at times because trying to keep them alive and this boat afloat was all I had in me. Their stories are each unique.

THE THIRTEEN
YEAR OLD

Nautas had turned thirteen on December 5, 2014. Just a mere twenty-four days before our earth was shattered by the Death Tsunami. He was staying at his friend's house that night for a sleepover. When he left our house everything was normal. When I picked him up at three a.m., nothing was normal. He got in the car, and we drove the few blocks home.

He was not Jay's biological son, but he was his son. Nautas was only eighteen months old when Jay and I started dating. He was two and a half when we married. Jay accepted him and took him in as his own. He loved my first born like he had been there from day one. Losing Jay was a huge and devastating blow to this young boy's heart.

Nautas struggled to process his grief. He turned to rage to cope. He began to rage through the house at times. He would scare his siblings and punch holes in doors. He didn't handle losing Jay well. He didn't know how to cope with all those big emotions. There was nothing I could really do to help because I could hardly complete a full thought and yet, I had four more kids and a business to run. I believe that Nautas felt like I had abandoned him in his grief.

Though he was only thirteen, he had to step up and help me with the family responsibilities in some ways. I would drop him off with my debit card and a grocery list and when he was finished gathering groceries for the family, I would come pick him up. He did the majority of our grocery shopping for years. I also had him mowing and working on other chores around the house.

We had some really hard moments over the next five years. He tortured us in many ways with his fits and screaming. I begged people to help me with him. Men. Men who were friends of ours, yet there wasn't an "ours" anymore. There was only a "me" and that didn't leave a lot of options. I asked his youth leader to help. He never showed up. I asked the pastor of our church, and he told me that I needed to contact the husbands of the women in my small group. I told the pastor that it wasn't my responsibility to contact the husbands of other women and that he should do that on my behalf. But he did not. I signed my son up for Big Brothers/Big Sisters, and they closed our "account" without ever even calling us. I called about military schools. Thirty thousand dollars a year with not an ounce of financial help available for widows. I called a boy's home, but my son had to be willing to go... and he wasn't. He wasn't willing to do anything really to ease the complexity of his situation. We went to anger management classes. I was hoping these would help him realize that he could manage his emotions better without the rage. It didn't work.

I bet you're wondering why I didn't put him in counseling? Of course I tried that! I took all the kids to a year of grief counseling, and he had his own separate counselors too. Nothing worked. It was chaos. It was awful.

There were days when I didn't know if I would survive these years with my son.

Nautas turned to marijuana when he was about fifteen to cope with his anger and grief. He and I have very different opinions on whether it has been beneficial or not. Even in my punk rock days, I was never one to accept drug use of any kind, so this was hard to navigate with my first-born son. I didn't want it to become a mountain between us, but it also wasn't acceptable behavior. These were very hard times, very hard years.

Today: We still have moments that we struggle. I am not sure that he has ever gotten over Jay's passing. He is smart and works hard. The struggle with his emotions is still very present at times. He is very funny and has the best wit! Wit. Wisdom. The Warrior Way. That is the path for him that God has set out. I look forward to watching him walk in his calling.

THE NINE YEAR OLD

Nyah was Jay's and my firstborn daughter. She was the best glue for our marriage. She and Jay were super close. I had pushed her to be close with him because I had always longed for that with my own dad, who passed away when I was four. Since we homeschooled, the kids were with Jay all the time.

I began to lean heavily on Nyah. Though she was only nine, she probably had to grow up the fastest of all the kids. Not long after Jay passed, we were at Burger King to grab dinner after an errand. I let the kids play to burn off some steam. As we were leaving, I put the girls into their car seats, and as I was closing their door, my driver side door closed and somehow locked my keys and my two babies in the car. I burst into tears! How had I put the girls in their seats and the doors were still locked? It was like I was in the Twilight Zone! I just stood there. Stunned. Devastated. The man I would call to help me was dead. My parents were out of town. My phone was next to my keys, and I didn't have brain cells functioning and didn't know a single phone number of anyone around me. I just wanted to melt and cease to exist. My brave daughter went to get help. Then, my sweet daughter and the manager walked out to my van and miraculously, they were able to pry my door open enough (because it had closed on its own, it wasn't fully closed into the door jam) to get it unlocked. I was so thankful!

She retracted to cope with her sadness and pain. When she was born, her animal was a snail. I picked animals for all my kids when they were born and maybe it was God helping me to understand them. The snail is a perfect representation of Nyah. When she is angry or hurt, she retracts. She will move into her snail shell for as long as it takes to process her emotions and feelings. She went very quiet. She processed her feelings that way for much of her teens. That made it a little bit difficult for me to know exactly how she felt. She was definitely a support I needed and trusted and relied on greatly. However, I never wanted her to have to be a supplement parent. I tried very hard to protect her from having to be the other grown up that I was now missing. That wasn't her role, and I wanted her to still be a child. It was a hard balance because I needed a lot of help with the babies.

She went through a period of time, at about fifteen years old, when she became masochistic and was cutting herself. So back to counseling for her, and she got on a mild antidepressant. She weaned herself when she was ready and able to handle all the complex emotions that come with puberty and grief. I was not alarmed at her cutting herself because I used to carve things into my hands when I was young. It might not have been exactly the same behavior, but we talked about it together. Some children might have severe issues with it, and may need intensive treatment, but she did not. She was a good student and a hard worker. She has always wanted to do things with excellence, and I believe she accomplishes that. She never seemed to allow what was happening in her heart spill over into her schooling.

Friendships were very complicated for her. She had friends turn their backs on her. She felt left out a lot. The complication with friendships seemed to be a continuing struggle for her as her heart was trying to mend. She was different. The other girls had their dads, she didn't. Like me when I was growing up without a dad, she felt that difference between herself and the other girls loud and clear.

Today: She just graduated high school and is very studious and responsible. She still retracts at times, but she expresses her feelings when she wants to. She is smart, creative, and kind. Sometimes she loves me, and sometimes she hates me, but I guess that is about what to expect from a teenage relationship. She is at the age to spread her wings, and so far, they are beautiful wings. God made music move in her soul, so I look forward to seeing how that plays out in her life as He blossoms that in her life.

THE SEVEN YEAR OLD

Hammuel (Hammy) Jordan has always been the defender of all things Jordan. He is Jay's only namesake. He was just a tender seven years old when his dad passed. Hammy loved going around with his dad. He has a memory that happened not long before Jay passed away; it was a very chivalrous moment of Jay's, and it has stuck with Hammy his whole life. Jay was very bold. One day, they were driving downtown and Jay saw an old man getting robbed. Jay drove his big old truck right up onto the curb and sidewalk and almost hit one of the robbers. They ran off and Jay hopped out to see if the old man was OK. They called the police and notified them about the robbery. Jay wasn't scared at all to help that old man when most people would've looked away. This made a great impact on Hammy.

He coped with the loss of his dad by quitting eating. If you actually could turn into the food that you eat, Hammy would be a ramen noodle. He lived on ramen noodles for years. Years!! That was the only food he would eat. I was concerned about it and talked to his pediatrician. He said it was a common grief expression and as long as he was eating something, not to worry. I did worry though because there are no health benefits to eating that stuff. But I just had to leave it up to God because we were all just surviving! Fortunately, he didn't turn into a ramen noodle, and eventually he started to eat a wider variety of foods. It took a long time though. I just had to give him grace.

He also coped by becoming very affectionate. He has always had a gentle, yet strong, personality. After Jay passed away, he needed a lot of hugs and affection. He would just come up to me and hug me. It was very casual, but very often. It was noticeably different from the way he was prior to the Death Tsunami. It was really sweet actually, and I always hugged him back. I don't know if it was a way for him to find comfort or if it was a way for him to validate that I was OK, but it was something that he needed for quite some time.

Today: He is a thriving high schooler. He loves soccer, which he has played since he was four. He is smart, witty, and compassionate. He loves to work and make money. He is easy going and loves his family. He eats a lot of food—and a variety. He is very tall like his dad, but slender like my brother. He has a deep passion for God, and a huge call on his life.

THE TWO YEAR OLD

Rebekah was so little when her dad passed. The next day, after she woke up, I told her what had happened. She told me in the sweetest voice, "My Poppa came and said bye to me." I burst into tears. She didn't know what she was saying to me, but I firmly believe that somehow, as he left here, he said goodbye to her.

She had a very hard time going to sleep after Jay passed. He was often the one to put her to bed, and she couldn't go to sleep. My friend, the kids call him Uncle D, is built much like Jay. He came every night for a few weeks to help her go to sleep. It was such an endearing and sweet time. Eventually, she would go to sleep again on her own.

She still grieves her dad sometimes with open tears and sadness. We process it together. Sometimes I will ask her questions or tell her a story about him when she is feeling sad. I remind her that it is very normal to miss her dad. Sometimes she will make comments about "not having a dad," and I remind her that she, indeed, does have a dad, he just isn't here on Earth.

I think it is hard for her to not have any memory of him but feel such a large gaping hole in her heart where he would belong.

Today: She is thriving and growing so big. She is funny and loves to sing. She is a fantastic artist and loves to write. She has so many of my same interests, and I love to watch her grow in her skills and talents. She is heading into her pre-teen years, so y'all pray for me! This girl is full of drama (like her dad)!!

THE EIGHT MONTH OLD

Shiloh was born this same year. "A little treasure" is what God called her. She was too little to show any signs of loss at the time. However, she mentions not getting to know her dad the most. She feels the loss deep on her inside and sometimes she grieves. She didn't start showing any signs of grief until she was about five.

Her older siblings have, at times, been impatient with her delayed grief. They do not understand that she literally didn't grieve for him at all at the time of his death. I have had to remind the older kiddos that she needs the same space to let herself feel the loss.

Today: She is her dad made over. I call her Jay Jordan Jr Jr. Jay was a Jr, so she is a Jr Jr. Out of all of our kids, she has so much of his personality and demeanor and his ability to love so deeply. She is hilarious and wickedly smart. She has incredible logic and is my techy kid. She loves video games. She is sensitive and doesn't take crap from anyone.

Chapter 5

MY STRUGGLE WITH RESENTMENTS

Oh man! I struggled so hard with resentments about being left alone with five kids. My kids weren't grown, and none of them were even close to fully self-sufficient. I was drowning under the weight of the family. My two littles needed all my time and attention. I resented that. I had barely any brain cells to draw from to start with, and then I had two little people that were always needing, needing, and needing. They were babies. They weren't trying to exhaust me, but they didn't have to try. I was already exhausted. The constant demands wore me down to a nub. My emotional energy was low to nearly nonexistent. Two babies, an eight month old, and a two year old will wear out someone with all their faculties. But me, I struggled to complete a full sentence, much less had the emotional wherewithal to handle this load.

Often in my journal entries to Jay, I would lament about how taxing it was. I didn't birth five kids by myself, and I was angry that I had been left to handle the load on my own. No one else could be me. No one else could guide these guys and help them navigate out of the dark valley of the Death Tsunami. I wanted to break things. I wanted to stand on my roof and scream the f-bomb as loud as I could. I wanted to die. I wanted to nuclear bomb my existence off of the planet more days than not.

I was so angry with God for leaving me here like this. I was so angry at Him for choosing to let Jay bail on me like that. I couldn't understand why God didn't take the deadbeat dads, the uninvolved dads, the indifferent dads. Why couldn't they be the ones that died? I saw plenty of unhealthy people just living right along in life, eating poorly and not taking care of themselves, yet Jay died at thirty-eight years old. He didn't take care of himself either, but why not take out some other someone who didn't take care of themselves *and* wasn't a good dad? Oh how I struggled with the unanswered "why" questions!

I was angry with God for taking my kids' dad. How dare He do the same thing to my kids that had happened to me? How dare he leave us here like this? Oh! I was so angry with God. I resented God! I resented that He hadn't written a different story. One that was more conducive to brain cells and less conducive to anger. Why did He have to continue to hurt me so much?

I have had a few prophecies that I stand on. One is that God told me, "Hang on and watch what I am going to do with this because it is going to blow your mind." So one night, as I was cursing God out, I said,"Oh yea! You're really blowing my mind!! Look at You just blowing my mind, God!"

He replied, "Watch your mouth, Stephanie."

Ugh. That wasn't what I wanted to hear at all. I wanted Him to take my sarcasm and anger and make it better! Why wouldn't he just FIX it all? Why couldn't He just take it all back and put us back like before? Like what felt like normal?!!

I'm sure if He had wanted to really have a good sit down with me and my pisspoor attitude, He would've answered me much like He did Job in the last few chapters. It would've been fitting—probably not fully comforting, but I would've gotten the point. However, telling me to watch my mouth was pretty dang sufficient to get me to shut it as far as sarcasm. My cynicism took much longer to dissolve.

I had to learn to forgive God. What felt like a slight against me truly had nothing to do with me at all. Jay was God's child and just a gift to me for the time I had him. I had to trust that God knew better than me, and though my heart took a long time to accept this truth, I was able to learn how to walk out that trust in my life. God promises that he will complete what he starts, and I had to trust that Jay was complete on this side of heaven. This is where autonomy shines even in a marriage covenant of oneness.

I was angry with Jay. I was so incredibly angry with Jay. How dare he leave me like this? How dare he bail on us? The audacity to go and die on his family. I didn't birth five kids by myself. How could he just leave me here by myself? I have always said that Jay broke my "misser." I didn't know you could miss someone that badly. I missed him so much. My anger was propelled by my broken heart of just missing him. I resented that he was gone but more that I missed him so much. Missing him was so prominent that it overshadowed everything.

There are some events and some days still, even over eight years later, that I miss him being here for the kids. Their birthdays, graduations, first _____, last

_____, and all the things you would share with your kids' father. Divorcees have the ability to be angry that the other person is there or isn't there in person, a widow/er doesn't have that option. Another distinct difference between the two.

Chapter 6

WIDOW

Throughout our marriage, Jay and I had many trials. We had a complex relationship. We both came from brokenness when God called us into this marriage. We built so much in our ten and half years together. We created a strong foundation that I couldn't see as we were building it. Each block with the name of Jesus written on it. If you look back in my prayer journals, I begged God to kill one of us no less than a hundred times. It was all out of foolishness. I was a fool to pen those words because I just wanted a reprieve from the difficulty of the relationship, not knowing what I was inviting.

Jay was a recovering addict and had had a relapse early in our marriage. Addiction, too, was a devastating spiritual storm in our early years of marriage. I am not sure that I ever got over the betrayal of that relapse and the damage that it did to us, my trust, and our family. The damage was vast and difficult to rebuild. However, we were sealed, and God encouraged me over and over again to just forgive him and love him. Earlier in this book, I shared that the Holy Spirit told me that if I left him I would always long for him. Not just told me, but actually let me feel the feeling in my chest. It was a deep aching. God consistently brought me back around to Jay and blessed our family, even though we were so messy.

Every year of our marriage we had some big event. We were either having babies, opening businesses, buying a house, building a new kitchen from a fire, or some big event. There was so much fullness in our marriage, so when death came, there was a lot to destroy. I have seen death take grown men to their knees and leave them writhing in the pain of life, never to resurface. I just had no idea how it would affect me when it took Jay.

During the immediate days after Jay passed away, while I had brain fog, I remember developing a crush on someone very quickly. I was stunned and appalled at myself and how that happened. I remember thinking,"What is going on? I don't even know this person, and my husband just died!" But I think it was my brain and heart trying to find somewhere to land. It had just been thrown around and tossed into the air unexpectedly. I believe that was a coping mechanism that really came out of left field, and one that I never would've expected.

Of course, when Jay was alive, and I had never been a widow, I used to wonder what being a widow would be like. My dad died when I was four; my mom had also been a widow. Death had always been present in my life, so thinking about what it would be like to have my spouse pass away wasn't a far thought. Jay being an addict, I had to accept during his relapse that him passing away could become a real possibility. Thankfully, that didn't happen, but accepting that is a step in healing from codependency. The only thing I could imagine was that I would miss him. Oh! How elementary that thinking was! I didn't have a clue what I was in for when I actually became a widow. A fellow widow friend said to me, "It is much heavier and way more awful than I expected," talking about her loss. I think that sums up my feelings well.

Widow. I hated that word. It felt like a betrayal and a lie. For the entire first year, I still felt VERY married. My heart was still married to Jay. He wasn't here, but I still felt like I belonged to him. Nothing felt right. Jay was a gigantic man. He was 6'3" and 390 pounds. You don't realize how accustomed you become to the amount of space that you and your spouse take up together. Everywhere we went, there was always the consideration of space for two. I always needed extra room with him. He took up a lot of space, physical space, and his personality was larger than life. He seemed too alive to die. He seemed too full of life to die. But die he did. And I became a widow. Stupid word, widow.

I began to understand why older literature refers to widows and widowers by that name as though it is a proper name. The sentence of an old literature book may read, "Widow Jane was our neighbor..." There was a distinction of who Jane was. She was no ordinary lady. She was not a wife, nor a miss, nor single, nor married, she was a widow. A completely separate class of humans. One who had met Death and survived. She was vulnerable and set apart because of her status. She was weaker. She was broken. She was sorting through the aftermath of the Death Tsunami and trying to rebuild what she could. She was the strongest, boldest survivor that looked totally defeated. Old literature seems to capture the essence of how culture treats you, except they don't verbally say anything. You just know that you are now different. You are no longer treated like a valid family.

Now you are pitiful and need to be pitied, yet there is a lack of compassion in it. Don't look her way, she may need something from you. Don't hover too long, she may rub off her death curse on you. Now you are a widow, given a title you hate and never asked for, but it is so very fitting. The Widow Stephanie. Took me many months to accept that name. The word itself ages you. Maybe not in physical appearance, but certainly by removing the innocence of life experiences.

Once I accepted it, I rejected the concept of being called a single mother. I wasn't a single mother!! I had not birthed five children by myself, nor had I been left. I was a widowed mother. That title comes along with so much more despair, depth of meaning, devastation. I was single, in that I wasn't married anymore, but I was not a single mother. There was no child support or man to call and yell at for not doing his part. There was no every-other-weekend-off or custody to deal with. It was just me and my children navigating a wretched place that we had been thrown into.

I've been divorced, and I've been widowed. They are not the same. They are not even close to the same. Do me a favor, next time you meet a widow, don't tell her you are divorced and understand because it is the same. Death does not tsunami your entire existence in divorce. There is no Shadow of Darkness with divorce. It. Is. Not. The. Same. Jesus never fought divorce, but He died to fight Death. Comparing divorce with death is shallow. Divorce is awful and devastating and does its own damage to one's heart. My divorce was a terrible, horrible, devastating experience, one I'd never want to go through again. However, many people choose to go through divorces over and over again. I don't know a single widow/

er that would ever in a million years hope to journey that road again and would fight every ounce of hell not to! Actually, it is one of the greatest fears to overcome after losing a spouse. The thought of losing another spouse is absolutely devastating and terrifying and prevents many people from ever remarrying. Divorce is propelled with emotions that you don't have with death. There are no resentments, level of anger, or disgust that even matter once death has come near. Those things almost dissipate in the initial tsunami wipe out that comes with death.

The title widow or widower should come with the utmost respect. Finding your way out of the darkest place that the Bible refers to, besides hell, is no easy feat, and for many, it takes years upon years to complete the journey. Some never make it out...which is partly the reason I am writing this book. If I can encourage just one person to keep walking through that journey, keep their eye on the pinprick of Light that is God, and come out on the other side, every minute, every letter I type, is worth it.

Chapter 7

HAUNTING?

I never felt haunted by Jay. He died in our house, in our bed actually. I slept fine. Heck, sleeping is how I survived for years. I napped regularly to shut my brain off and heal. I'm sure there is some fancy psychology behind that, but I just know that that was a major coping mechanism for me. Sleep was as critical as breathing in those early years of widowhood. Chewing gum was next. I have no idea the amount of gum—pounds I'm sure—that I chewed through to work out my anxiety and stress. Sleep and gum, my coping mechanisms and life savers.

Typically we equate the term "haunting" with something scary or disturbing. I never felt that my innate awareness of Jay's presence, even after he was gone, was scary or disturbing. There was no sense of his lurking. It didn't still feel like he was there. It was just that my mind had memorized Jay's presence in the home. I could still hear Jay walking down the hallway. Did you know every person has a sound unique to them? It may be their keys on their belt loop or the way their feet shuffle. Maybe they always hit the same place on the door frame. Jay had many things that represented him in the house. His sound was certainly one. I would lay in my room and would look at the door, knowing any minute he would round the corner because I could hear him coming. My ears teased me.

I would pull into the driveway everyday and expect to see him standing there to help me get the kids out of the car. Yet, every day, he wasn't there. I could see him, but he wasn't there.

I had a vision in my mind of looking in the rearview mirror, and there was Jay. The kids and I were still moving forward, and he was standing there watching us as we went away. I could see this in my mind for a very long time. It was a vision of what was happening, and I couldn't stop it. I couldn't turn around and pick him back up. I wasn't in control of the car I was in. Then one day, he was no longer in the rearview, and I just had to look forward.

Because of his wide hips, he left markings on all the door frames where his belt would scratch against it as he walked through. For the longest time, those scratches were endearing, and then they became heartbreaking. I could hear it as I walked past them. I remembered being agitated at him for scratching the door frames. Then somehow, that didn't seem so important.

He was tall and did metal work. We had a business named Exodus Iron and Forge. He made some incredibly beautiful iron pieces. His hands often had mechanic dirt or metal dust on them, and he would raise his hands above his head and rest them on the frame of the living room. I left his fingerprints there until about a year ago. I considered framing them and leaving them there, but as the years have gone on, I have learned to accept that I have to let Jay go. I can't leave him, or my family along with him, frozen in time.

I have had dreams about Jay. There were some in the beginning of him asking me to not be mad at him because God needed him. He always looked amazing. I believe he was in his perfected self. He was in his heavenly form, and it was glorious. He looked like himself, with his style, but he was radiant and full of joy and healthy, and it encouraged me.

After a few years, I had dreams that I was trying to find him and couldn't. I was very angry during these dreams. I felt betrayed, which is, I am sure, how I felt inside. The final dream I had was after I met the guy that I intend to have a future with. Jay came and said goodbye to me. It was a sweet and pleasant dream. I didn't realize at the time that it would be the last time.

I could always hear Jay talk to me on my inside. Not the same as the Holy Spirit talking to me, but kind of similar. I could hear him cheering me on to keep going and saying that everything we believe about Jesus and death and afterwards is real. I could hear him chastise me when I dated a long-time family friend who is a complete jerk. I always felt him close by until I started dating a man I plan to be with forever. I could feel Jay's love for me deep in my heart. It is still there. I know that he loved me deeply to my very core. Jay's love was a propelling force for me when he was alive, and it has been a lifeline saving grace for me since he died. His love was so genuine and complete that I know without a shadow of a doubt that it has sustained me in very low places in life.

This year, 2023, is the first time I have ever felt haunted by him. Not because of him, but because of me. I can't let him go in some ways. My kids long to know him and talk to him. His loss being a shadow over every moment: birthdays, graduations, celebrations. There is always the enormous missing. I used to say that Jay "broke my miss-er." I never knew you could miss someone so much. I miss not being able to share the kids with him. These are the moments we longed for and dreamed about. Our kids are getting to the ages where they are now fully formed people with their own brains and personalities, and he is missing it.

Though Jay has never haunted me, I fight the urge to never let him go. Letting him go is the only way to keep moving forward.

Chapter 8

SURVIVAL

Looking back on those years, I am always in awe and still can cry about how we survived that time. I don't know if I inherently had some survival mechanisms built in or if God was just so gracious to walk me through it all, or maybe it was a combo of the two. I have the ability to roll with punches, and I am not much of a habitual person, so change is one of my favorite things. Most of the time I love change. This was not a change that I loved. However, because I don't get stuck in the idea that things have to be done in a certain way (all you habitual people are melting about now), I am able to modify quickly.

One thing that I did the very first month after he passed away was choose to wear the same exact pair of pants every single day. Yes! I washed them...some. I was suffering from major decision fatigue, and I didn't want to have to think about what I put on my body. Decision fatigue is a very real issue when someone has more decisions to make than possible. I wasn't capable of sorting through so much information and making a decision for every single little thing. So I made one decision and stuck with it. Did anyone notice? Nope. I doubt it. However, it was a lifesaver for me. It seems like this is trivial, but when your brain has vacated the premises and is in perpetual hibernation mode, along with an overload of decisions to be made, along with formerly close-friends-and-family-now-vultures trying to steal all your husband's stuff, a decision like wearing the same pants helps keep you sane.

I realized about a month in that my brain had a dam of everyday life issues. I wasn't telling anyone what was happening in my day-to-day events. I had had that person for over ten years. What are we going to have for dinner? What did you do today? How was your day? Did you go to the grocery store? Did you put gas in the car? What is that smell? I mean, any of the mundane things you say to your person every day are gone. Poof! It's just a void. However, your brain holds onto that stuff because you used to filter it, and there was a steady and consistent flow of thought. Jay and I were both motor-mouths and talked a lot. There was constant conversation in our home.

Just to give you an example, my oldest son went to spend the night at a friend's house, and he was talking to the kid's mom. She asked him, "You sure are able to talk a lot. Does your family talk a lot?"

He answered, "Yes. We talk all the time."

We talk a lot in our house.

To counter the void, I started to journal the everyday things to Jay. I would write the things down out of my head. Frustrations, casual conversations, sadness, and funny things were all a part of the journaling. I wrote every day for the first year. This was so important for me. I never realized how dependent I was on having those little conversations with him, but once he was gone, my head became so full of them that it was making me a bit agitated. I am an external processor, so losing my ability to process was very difficult.

It is also hard when no one even cares what you do in a day. You don't know how much it matters that someone asks you about your day until it just disappears. I didn't have to go home at a certain time, and if I had my kids with me, no one was waiting on me. I didn't have to tell anyone where I was going, when I was going, or how long I would be gone. That may sound amazing, like complete freedom for some people, but it grows sad and lonely when all in the house is quiet, and it is just you. On a typical day when I got home from work, I was thrust immediately into mom mode, and I had all the kids in my face with all their needs all at once. I had to instill a rule that they could not ask for anything, and I mean *anything*, for at least twenty minutes after I got home. The instant barrage of their needs, after having served my staff and clients' needs all day, would send me into a tizzy quite quickly.

Twenty minutes to just say "hello" and greet each other, and for me to change out of my work clothes, gave me enough ability to move into the house mode. It is amazing how many needs can be gathered by five people every day. "Can I have _____?" became a nemesis question. If they asked me within the first twenty minutes, the immediate answer was no. They learned quickly that I wasn't kidding about needing that time to settle and shift.

I used to call my mom every day on the way to and from work, before life changed. We would talk about anything and everything. After death stole my emotional energy and brain cells, all the phone calls stopped. I was almost angry if someone wanted to engage me in a phone conversation. I missed talking to my mom, but the silence was more enticing. I found myself lost in my head a lot. Trauma seems to cause the effect of being lost in the head—all the thoughts and emotions that you are trying to sort and organize and work through. There was so much happening in my head, but forming a complete sentence out of my mouth was nearly impossible.

One day my mom and one of her friends were at my house cleaning. My mom asked me where to put certain items. I told her, completely ingenuously, to put cups in the fridge and food on the couch! I was irritated with her for asking me questions, but I was more irritated that I couldn't even answer them logically! She said,"You are clearly not doing OK. I think you should go take a nap, and I will take the kids to go get lunch." That was the best statement she could have made because my brain was in overload. I was having to use energy and mind power, and both were in very short supply.

I wanted to move. My kids did not. I chose to stay in our home so that the kids would continue to have stability. I knew that it was important to them to maintain living here where Jay was, and I wanted them to feel as safe as possible. People suggested that I get some roommates or go to live with my parents for a while, but all those choices, although from good hearts, couldn't have been further from what sounded like a good idea than living in hell itself. I was not about to bring people into our lives that we would have to be considerate of when we were just surviving. There are only so many stressors that one can handle before he or she completely breaks, and I am fairly certain that had I brought someone else into my home, I would've cracked and broken into a million sharp pieces. It would have been messy. I am thankful that God provided for us during these days.

MIRACLES AND THANK YOUS

There were many miracles that we experienced during this crazy time. Being able to stay in our home and being able to keep stability for my kids was one of the greatest ones! I never knew how much God was setting us up to be able to maintain our lives.

God's faithfulness was so rich and deep in the grief season. I had no regrets. There wasn't a sorry left unsaid between Jay and I. In the miraculous healing that God gave us in the months prior to his death, He led us to say our sorrys and speak our hearts until they were healed. There was nothing left to be said. God spared me and my heart from the utter devastation that was sure to follow had I allowed my pride to be the leader. He had warned me that I would always long for Jay, and He was absolutely correct. Had I met Death without those months of healing and preparation, I would have struggled to ever get my head above the waters I felt like I was drowning in in widowhood. A precious gift God gave me, which He knew I needed, was peace and grace between us. THANK YOU GOD!

My salon should have closed. My salon should have crumbled and fallen apart, but it didn't. Truly, it thrived because it was God's way of providing for us. He kept all the balls rolling, and I just kept showing up. He gave me wisdom to make decisions, and I leaned heavily on my staff, who thankfully, showed up to the game and did incredible work. I was only in my second year of business when Jay died, and my landlord told me that he would do anything to help keep my business open. He was an incredible gift. He taught me business and money concepts and encouraged me. I know that God put me in that space for that season. I closed my salon store front in 2020, completing my seven year prophecy, to career shift into author, teacher, and speaker. When I called him to tell him I was going to shut down, he offered me a year's worth of free rent. I was in the best place of my entire career and could have built an incredible future, but God has other plans, and I am here for it. THANK YOU!

People fed us for six to seven months. Someone, I don't even know who, set us up a meal train, and it just kept going. Every other day for months, people showed up gracefully with food to feed my large crew. Sometimes we would laugh because, though I have five kids to feed, the two littles were so young that they didn't eat much. Sometimes it was hard to eat all the food! I was so humbled by the love that people gave. It was a huge relief for me to not have to come up with food or dinners or lunches even. Food can be such a drag to have to figure out when things are normal, but I think we would've starved at times had people not brought us food. One friend bought us a years' membership to Shipt. If you were a part of feeding us and keeping us alive, THANK YOU!

Someone generously paid for our entire homeschool co-op year for the next school year. It was anonymous, so I still don't know who, but it was such a huge gift! That was another thing that I didn't have to think about and another way of provision that took some of the load off of me. My homeschool director was also very gracious! I was always supposed to be on campus and fully engaged if my kids were there , but she knew that I was running a company and also had other kids that may need attention. She always gave me the grace to be where I needed to be and allowed my kids to be able to be involved in the co-op. Moms would look out for my kids when I needed to handle something or had a sick kid and couldn't attend. This group was such a vital part of being able to survive that season. They rallied around me and held us. I am forever grateful. THANK YOU!

I went to California to see my brother, the Rock Doc, defend his dissertation thesis to get his doctorate in geology. On the way home they messed up my flight. I got a one-way ticket voucher to make up for the airline's mistake. I had no idea what I was going to do with a one-way ticket. Don't get me wrong, I would have loved at times to disappear and never return, but that was not going to happen because I didn't have six one-way tickets, and I would never have left my kids.

Around this time, our minivan was starting to have some mechanical problems. I started looking for a new van and found one in Chicago that was perfect! It was exactly what I wanted. Lo and behold, I had this one-way ticket. So I organized it with the company, flew to Chicago, bought my van, and drove it home. I was able to visit some friends on the way home, and it was really an incredible trip. I stayed overnight at a friend's house in Louisville,Kentucky, that was exactly halfway on my trip. I stopped the next day, again halfway to arriving at home for day two, to eat lunch with a friend in Nashville. It was like God had made that ticket happen just for me because He was making a way for me to get the van that I didn't even know I was going to be looking for. THANK YOU!

I went to a grief group for a year after Jay passed. These people were so helpful and instrumental in my healing. Jay had prayed the entire summer before he passed that God would heal the little girl inside of me. Eight months after he died, God answered his prayer in incredible ways. I learned so much about myself, my hurts, my damage; and God healed it. I was able to be restored, just like God had promised me with that scripture when He called me to marry Jay. I had washed in the Jordan and been renewed in my heart. This group gave me the grace to process and grieve and experience miracles! THANK YOU!

One friend set up a GoFundMe that raised $10,000 for us. That money was so helpful to get his cremation and urn paid for. It helped cover daycare costs that increased, exponentially when I enrolled Shiloh. Jay also had some friends who put on a live punk rock concert in his honor for our benefit. It was awesome to see people come out and support that cause. They also made a memory book in which they shared memories about Jay. It was hard for many to come up with PG-rated stories about Jay because he was a rascal. One day I will share the memory book with the kids, and they can laugh about how many comments are made about there not being any PG-rated stories about Jay. THANK YOU!

My lifelong best friend, Robbie, went grocery shopping for me for an entire year! She would go once a week. I think she might have even paid for them. If not all of them, some of them. She helped me with things around my house. She just showed up, diligently, every week. She came to see that whatever needs we might have could be met. She would help cook food. She didn't disappear after the first three months like many of the others. Nope, this girl, my rock, came to my house and helped for a year. This trait is something I have always admired so much about Robbie. She is solid and dependable. She is an anchor when my life hits storms. THANK YOU!

Every single Saturday for four years, I needed childcare so that I could be at work. One challenge of being a hairstylist is the Saturday work schedule. Regular daycares aren't open on Saturdays, and most people have things to do. Babysitting someone else's kids is usually not in the plans. I had eight amazing Saturday Angels, that is what I call this group of ladies, that watched my whole crew for me. I would plan one to two months out at a time so that no one had to watch them more than once every other month. They were always ready and willing to take a Saturday and love on my kids. They would take them to do fun things, and include them in all sorts of fun activities, and along with their families. THANK YOU!

All of my salon clients were so patient with the process of my grieving and my need to take care of my children. My children became regulars with me at work, and no one seemed to mind. I would struggle, sometimes, with tears. I couldn't always hold them in. My eyes would betray me and let all my feelings out. I had many people come to support me because they knew that I was now supporting five children on my own. They were generous and kind. In some ways, they seemed protective of me and the journey I was walking. I probably wouldn't have made it, especially financially, if my clients hadn't continued to have grace and care for us during many years. THANK YOU!

Thank you to all the people who showed up in big and small ways. The guys that helped lock up the workshop in my backyard that people were robbing of Jay's valuables, the people who cleaned my house, and the grief group that helped me to heal. Thank you to all the people who cared about us, our story, our journey. I can't remember all of the situations and the things that happened and who all stepped in, but God knows. God saw. He is clear in the Bible (James 1:27) that taking care of widows and orphans is the only way to show your religion and everyone who showed up did an incredible job!

BOUNDARIES

I could not have survived my situation without boundaries. I was climbing an uphill battle in quicksand, and I wasn't about to let someone make it harder than it already was. I was fighting to keep sane and for my own life. Every single day was a survival challenge, and when others created situations that made anything harder, I would have to put my foot down.

People tend to overstep when there is so much wide-open vulnerability. I needed people. I couldn't do it without people, and that can make for a mess in relationships. I really had to learn how to set boundaries. My tag line became,"If it isn't helpful, it isn't helpful." By that I mean, people would think they were helping me, and then it caused stress or strife, which then wasn't helpful at all. So truly, it was never helpful to begin with. I had to stop those types of situations by having better, clearer, and straightforward communication with people. It wasn't comfortable really and it, at times, led into conflict, but it kept me more sane.

One example is my stepdad was doing my mountain of laundry. The amount of laundry my six people could make was pretty insane. I had a baby and two year old who were constantly physically growing, and along with seasonal changes and the incessant messes that they made, their laundry needs were endless. It was ridiculous. I was getting hand-me-downs left and right (whoop whoop for the hand-me-downs!). They were life savers, but then I had to sort and pack and do all the things that hand-me-downs require in order to become useful. Huge bags full of clothes aren't typically beneficial unless you actually know what is inside them.

So, my stepdad was trying to be helpful and tackle some of the mountain of laundry. However, when it came time to retrieve that laundry, he wanted me to come to retrieve it from his house, which is about thirty minutes away from my house. It is also in the opposite direction from my work to go to his house instead of mine. When I left work, I had five children to feed, teach (homeschool), take care of, and get ready for the next day of heaping mounds of life. Despite how grateful I was for his help, I didn't have the time, energy, or ability to go and get the laundry. He got angry with me and chastised me. Then I told him that I appreciated him doing the laundry, but in the future I didn't need him to do the laundry if it was going to cause more issues. It wasn't help. It wasn't helpful. It caused undue stress.

So was I being ungrateful? I mean, he was helping me. This is where boundaries and codependency can get messy. I have written a whole book on boundaries called *Believing in Boundaries*, if you want to learn more about codependency and boundaries. If I was operating out of codependency, I would have felt guilty and bent over backwards to make sure that I could get the clothes. It would've been to my own detriment. It would have cost me a lot of valuable time and energy that I didn't have to give. So yes, his intention was to help me, but I needed it to be helpful by not costing me time and energy that was already depleted.

My parents and I had to come to many new understandings during this season of my life. We had to navigate many changes. There was one particularly dramatic situation that was maybe one of the hardest boundaries to set. My parents had always been really involved with my children and sometimes there were lines that were crossed. This particular situation involved me disciplining my oldest son, who was full of rage and somewhat out of control, and they intervened in an attempt to mollify the situation. The problem is that it created a bigger problem between me and my thirteen-year-old son. Our relationship was already strained, and he was being very disrespectful. I told them to back off and stay out of it (a boundary), but they couldn't help themselves. So, I got angry and abruptly left their home, which made my kids scream and my parents cry, but I made myself very clear that I wasn't going to tolerate anyone making things more difficult for me and my kids. Afterwards, they did well hearing me. I appreciated that. From then on, they were willing to keep out of my parenting where they weren't invited, but that was a really difficult boundary to establish.

There wasn't a single relationship that I was in that I didn't have to set boundaries in some way. I had to become very protective of everything. I was teetering on the very fine tip of balance. Just about anything could have thrown me off-kilter and into a tailspin. I really didn't have the emotional energy to fight with people or deal with relational repair. Every day was survival, so it was important to make sure that everything went as smoothly as possible. Meeting the needs of so many people and having so many moving parts to keep the machine going is too much on its own, but if I allowed complications to arise, even one little glitch in the well-oiled machine, we would have fallen apart.

I am sure in some ways I became hard. I definitely became unapologetic for survival. I learned to be tough and hard, when necessary, to protect us. I would remove or block obstacles and/or people that became difficult. This may not have become one of my finer character traits that I acquired during the widowhood journey, and sometimes I think that I haven't been able to let go of this part of me. I am thankful that I had learned so much about boundaries before this time of my life. Boundaries were a huge lifeline during this season, and I believe they protected us well.

HOLIDAYS

Holidays are one of those crazy times after widowhood. There is still an anticipation of good times, mostly based on memories, but it is usually a time cloaked in dread. The first holiday we went through was New Year's Eve. It was a mere two days after his passing. Some sweet friends came by and supervised my kids while they shot fireworks. I sat in the fog.

The next holiday was Valentine's Day, and this one, though Jay and I didn't make a huge deal out of it normally, had a ton of weight and sadness to it. It was the first Valentine's that I didn't have that special someone in over a decade. Some other single ladies and myself got together and made dinner and had margaritas and celebrated. It was actually quite a pleasant night and ended up being completely survivalable. My bestie, who was actually married, sacrificed her V-day with her husband to come and spend mine with me. I thought that was so sweet, hanging out with us now-unhitched gals.

Next came Shiloh's first birthday. This was a tough day. I had a friend, who was raised in her parents' bakery, who made incredible cakes. Jay always carried Shiloh in the bibs of his overalls. Everyone would always comment on it. Before it was common or cool for dads to wear their babies, Jay did it in his style, like he did everything, and wore her tucked in the front of his overalls. So my friend made her first birthday cake from a pic of her dad carrying her in his bibs. I burst into tears when I saw the cake. It was the sweetest thing and the best way we could have had him present at that moment.

Father's Day was coming, and I didn't exactly know what I was going to do for it. It was, of course, a touchy subject. I decided that we would get green balloons and write messages to him and send them up into the sky. That is exactly what we have done every year since 2015. Some years the kids will let me see what they write and some years, they won't. I never pry because I think it is special for them to have privacy at that moment. It is their chance to celebrate him the only way they can.

We made it through the first year without him, one dreaded holiday after the next. I remained celebratory for my kids, though I don't think I really felt it. We celebrated our special Jordan Christmas Eve tradition, with pj's and Jesus' birth story. Jay was definitely gone but not forgotten. I actually got very ill that night and wasn't sure that I was going to be able to participate. Fortunately, I pressed through. We have continued this sweet night every year, and I always think of him. We started it together, with this big crew that we have, and the kids count on it. They look forward to it, and it encourages my heart that they love the family bond that night represents.

I have learned that there is no right or wrong way to celebrate or not celebrate when you are grieving. The important thing is to survive the holiday. Just live another day, and it gets easier to handle as the years move along. The sting of missing that person is always present, and that is OK. You may need to set strong boundaries in place around your holidays and how you and your children operate with other family and friends.

Surviving each day was the primary goal. We did. We survived. There were days that I barely got out of bed. There were days that I woke up five minutes before I had to leave for work. But I got up! I went. I showed up. Despite myself, my broken heart, my devastation and my longing to die, I showed up. Every. Single. Day. I resented that there was no reprieve from it all. No reprieve from life, work, kids, business, bills, and all the daily, weekly, and monthly tasks that life requires to function. Where was my escape? I needed an escape. At least I thought I did. Instead, slowly but surely, God was a lamp unto my feet and a light on my path, and He guided me out of that devastatingly dark place of the Valley of the Shadow of Death. One day, years into the journey, seven to be exact, I walked out of the shadow and back into the light again. I woke up and everything had changed. Morning, from my very long nightmare, had come.

Chapter 9

WHAT DID I LEARN ABOUT DEATH?

MIRACLES, RESTORATION, AND HEALING

I'm going to dig in a little deeper about the healing that came with Jay's death, where God renewed me as a young child. I think of all the miracles that took place, this is the one that is going to be what I scream from the mountain tops. It is glorious redemption and incredible healing.

You'll have to know a little of my backstory first. My father died on February 9, 1982. I had just turned four years old the December before. He died in a car accident with another woman. It was how my mom found out he was having an affair. My mom and I became widows at the same age, thirty-seven. I always thank her for the good legs, but she could've kept the widowhood to herself. I hated my dad pretty much my whole life. What a low-down craphead to have cheated on his family and died like that. Obviously, he didn't didn't care about me. Welcome abandonment issues. Welcome anger. Welcome rage. Welcome hatred.

These were things I had carried with me all my life. For a variety of reasons, I didn't have a good relationship with my step-dad growing up, so the fact that my dad had bailed on us and was a jerk meant that I hated men. I didn't know how that was going to play out in my life. I was so young when all these things happened that I just shelled up my heart. I desperately longed to be loved but was terrified and didn't trust men at all. This is how I ended up married to an alcoholic for my first marriage and became a survivor of domestic violence. I was broken and he was broken, and we loved each other. It was a nightmare. After we divorced, the beginning of this book takes place, and I marry Jay. We were also broken. The difference is that we had God at the center of our relationship.

Jay didn't care how broken I was, he loved me anyway. He did begin to see, or God began to show him, how broken I was, and that is when he began to pray for me. All those issues, the anger, rage, and hatred, were showing up with a vengeance in our marriage. I hated him, but maybe more I just hated what he represented. Every day he started to pray that God would heal the broken little girl inside of me. The one that had gotten tangled up in snares in the Valley of the Shadow of Death the first time I visited at four years old. I couldn't see my way out then and pieces of me made camp in the darkness. So God used Jay to bring me back there, but this time I was armed with Jesus and could see the light that would lead me out.

Eight months after Jay died, while I was in my Grief Share class, I had an epiphany in which I was not given the grief of a daughter with a dead father; instead, I was given the grief of a cheated-on spouse because that was my mom's experience. My mind was blown! This epiphany spiraled into a few months of a journey of God taking my shattered family from 1982 and putting it back together in 2015. I learned to accept that my dad didn't abandon me because he died. I had to forgive him for making poor decisions that were selfish. Fortunately, by the time this season of healing came, I had certainly done enough stupid things in my life that if I had died while doing them, I would not have wanted them to constitute the full summation of who I was. My dad's affair was the only thing that I had ever known about him really. His biggest, greatest, stupidest moment became the summation of who he was in my head my whole life, and that fueled my hatred towards him and all men. As God revealed to me that he was so much more than that moment, that sin, and that I was wanted by him and that I was his daughter, whom he loved, I was able to understand my place. A place I had never had before, which was a daughter, loved by her father.

All the places that had snared my heart at the tender age of four, were now lit up by my Heavenly Father so that I could unsnare my heart and heal. Healing these areas were the darkest corners of sadness and devastation for me, but in the most glorious way, God walked me gently through each place, and gave me revelation that has caused revolution in my heart. Walking life with Jay Jordan, my equivalent of washing in the Jordan seven times, allowed God to renew my young little girl's heart. I was healed and whole. A beloved daughter able to forgive her sinful father, who loved her and wanted her. I believe to this day if my dad had known that he wouldn't have made it home from that trip, he would have never gone. But should've, could've, would'ves don't allow us to move forward, and it was time to move forward in the Valley.

WE WERE NEVER MEANT TO TASTE DEATH

We were never meant to taste death. Our original design was to live in peace and harmony and to subdue creation. God designed us in His image and to be in unison with Him. However, when the Knowledge of Good and Evil entered onto Earth, death was part of the good-and-evil knowledge. Death came along with sin, which means we weren't designed to know it.

It is the only "natural" thing that happens to us that we are not able to reconcile. Being born, which is the most insane thing a person can go through, doesn't traumatize us. Growing into an adult person from a child doesn't traumatize us. We were made to experience these things, and they are natural and normal. But death, that is a completely different story. When someone we love dies, we can't reconcile it. We are utterly devastated and our hearts search for all the answers. If the death is caused by another human, we are furious and demand justice because it was evil. If it is caused by an illness, we want answers about why it didn't get better. If death happens to a child, it feels like an injustice. If death happens to a father of five, it seems utterly and completely unfair. Because death is an invasive spiritual element that we weren't created for, yet we all deal with it, we have to reckon with it at some point in our lives. I urge you to have God when you do! Death summoned me so many times during the early years of widowhood especially. Life was so hard. I struggled with suicidal tendencies so many times. All the lies in my head about no one cares, no one was there, no one would miss me, tore at my heart. I had to learn to fight it with truth. I've fought suicidal tendencies my whole life, but in that dark valley, death being so close, it didn't seem like I could get away. Maybe the death of my father opened the door to Death calling me. I can't ever remember a time that I didn't want to die. God was the only one who kept me here. Let God minister to you when you are summoned by Death, or when you are walking through that terribly dark valley. Otherwise, it may be a place that you will find that you don't come back from.

Why can't people come back? Because death is the Great Nothing. It annihilates everything. It will completely destroy mental, physical, spiritual, and emotional health. It arrives so very stealthily and then...they are just gone. The person you loved, the one you built your life with, or depended on, is gone. Poof! That was it. Everything you've ever said was all you could ever say. Everything you never said, now you can never say. Our eternal spiritual makeup cannot reconcile with that, and we feel robbed.

The beauty of Jesus Christ is that He built the redemption bridge with the cross. He died, in the same pattern that we do, in human form, so that He could go and conquer Death and Hades. Death is such a powerful spiritual force that God Himself had to defeat it on our behalf. Now Jesus holds the key to Death and Hades (Revelation 1:18), and we no longer fear death happening to us (1 Corinthians 15:54-57). We are able to rejoice that death is no longer the end story for those who have accepted Jesus as Lord and Savior. For a Christian, death is now only an usher. Death ushers us into our after life, but it has no control over us. As a matter of fact, the Bible refers to Christians as being asleep (1 Thessalonians 4:13). It never refers to a believer as being dead. That term is only used for nonbelievers. I believe that "being dead" is a loaded dual statement. I believe it is referring to a physical death of the body but more importantly a spiritual death. This spiritual death is the issue with spending eternity in hell. Hell is an eternal separation from God. If you've been thrown into the Valley of the Shadow of Death, you have experienced the closest thing on Earth to having a droplet taste of what hell will be like. There will be weeping and gnashing of teeth (Matthew 13:42) just like how we mourn after the death tsunami has come. Death and Hades reside together, so Death is an usher to Hell if people are not redeemed in Christ. The very purpose of Jesus coming was to disrupt the spiritual forces of evil, create redemption for all mankind (Jews and Gentiles), and show us the way to live.

We will never get away from death. It is something that will happen to us and to those we love. Christians need to make sure that they do not live in fear of death because of the hope that we have in Jesus. We need to show the world that we can be thrown into the Shadow of Death with the Death Tsunami and come out alive and rebuild our lives. It is not easy. It is not work that I could've done without God. It has been the absolutely hardest journey I have ever taken. There has been beauty for ashes every step of the way. There is a light, a pin prick of light, in that dark valley. It is God. Set your eyes on Him, and let him lead you out.

You may be like me, where death has ensnared pieces of you in the dark valley before, and now you face it
again. You aren't alone. God is there! Jesus made sure of
it. You will have to do the work of walking through it.
You may feel weak and broken, probably because you
are, but you won't stay there. This journey is a spiritual
domain, not a physical one, so it will happen without
your ability to control it. It is OK to not be OK and to
do it your way. There is no right or wrong way to walk
through the valley, just keep walking.

DEATH CHANGES
ALL YOUR RELATIONSHIPS

One thing I never considered prior to becoming a widow is how much your relationships change. I just always thought that once you had "couple friends," they were always your friends. That was foolish thinking. Those friendships seemed to almost vanish immediately. Invitations to go eat after church, gone. Invitations to the holiday cookout, poof, gone. It was like I had become invisible. I clearly wasn't invisible, I was the Widow Stephanie. The perpetual rain to any living person's parade, which might actually be true when I look back on it, but it still would've been nice to be included.

I actually had a very foolish pastor say to me, "I'd like to think that if I died that my friends would take care of my wife." Yessir. I bet you do. But the chances are, they won't, and you'll be too dead to know. Yep, this is the same pastor who told me to call other women's husbands to get needs met like grass mowing and such. Foolishness. Not an ounce of curiosity to learn about this ugly hellhole called widowhood. The club no one wants to be a part of. The club of the unseen and unwanted. The Death Tsunami survivors club. Sheesh, it's a terrible club! Most of Jay's friends and family, the ones he brought into our relationship, haven't ever had anything to do with me or my kids. Maybe life just got too busy. Maybe they didn't like me. Maybe we reminded them of sadness. Maybe... who knows? But they were gone.

This fulfilled a prophecy I had gotten in 2005. I was pregnant with Jay's and my first baby. I was visiting a church, and it was a divine appointment set up by God. The prophet told me many things that night, but one thing he told me was,"The church will never support you. On behalf of the church, I apologize." I was confused by this. I thought he was referring to our R.I.O.T. ministry. It was so out of the box, but we had had a ton of support. Fast forward to a few years after Jay passed away, and I was reading a post on Instagram. A famous Christian teacher had posted that we need to keep "family" business within the church and not spread it out to the world. I responded that it is hard as a widow with five kids and the church is nowhere to be found. There were many comments about large congregations and blah, blah, blah. I wasn't in a large congregation at the time, but that wasn't the main thing that caught my eye. Nope. It was a South African lady who posted,"On behalf of the church, I apologize for us not supporting you." And immediately I was like,"Oh my goodness! That is what God was warning me about all those years ago!" God was telling me that He already knew that the church wouldn't support me. I felt like God was so close to me at that moment. I was able to straighten up and walk a bit further in the dark valley, knowing that my Father already knew what was happening and had warned me before, so many years before.

I seemed to become a project for many friends who didn't disappear. I am probably to blame for that. I was needy. I was climbing up a mountain in quicksand with five kids in tow. I don't know if ten people a day could have made a dent in all the things I needed, but I would've been game to try it out. I'm sure some of my friends dreaded that I needed help every time they saw me. I appreciate the ones that didn't bail.

I think some people would have liked to remain friends, but I was unavailable. My emotional energy was not just depleted, it was annihilated. The Death Tsunami had wrecked every ounce of emotional energy I had. I didn't have the ability to be a friend or care about anything more than breathing. Once I regained my breath, I was still drowning. I remember telling some people that I felt like I had been cast down into the depths of the ocean, and I was swimming upwards as fast and hard as I could, but I felt like I might drown because I wasn't gonna crest the surface in time, and I couldn't breathe. It is hard to have friendships when you are drowning in something that no one can see, no one can control, and no one can fix. This part of friendship doesn't give our controlling tendencies warm fuzzy feelings. Walking alongside a widow is dark, ugly, messy work that drags on for years, sometimes many many years.

Every relationship that I had prior to the day that death came was touched. I was different. They were different. Nothing remained the same. I became a nicer version of me, one that was more patient, more kind, more compassionate. I had seen hell and was coming back from it, but I didn't have any interest in trivial malarkey that I now knew was a waste of time and energy. I had to work through forgiving God, forgiving Jay and forgiving myself. There was no time to worry about others in that life space. It took me years, four, maybe five, years before I had enough emotional energy to revisit any relationship that got tangled in the storm of death. By then, some of them were so distant that it didn't seem like there was a point to the revisiting. I accepted that the future would hold a different set of everything, like friends and maybe a spouse, in my life. I am still in the process of reconnecting with people.

THE ART OF BECOMING UN-ONE

This is the hardest thing I have ever endured in my life. The Bible, in Ephesians 5:31, says that a man is to leave his father and mother, and when he marries his wife, they become one flesh. When Jay and I married, I was such a mess that I didn't feel bonded to him for nearly two years after we got married. Those first two years I was very skeptical about whether we were even going to make it. Once we bonded, once God had sealed us together, that was it. We were definitely one flesh. I always appreciated how our children were a representation of that oneness. We always loved each other and were completely dedicated to each other. There was absolutely no one else, and we knew that we wouldn't have been able to separate. We were one.

After Jay died, I had to learn the art of becoming un-one. That is what I called my day-in and day-out surviving. I had to learn to live without him. I was only a Jordan because he was a Jordan. Who was I now? What did the name Jordan mean to me? Did I want to still be a Jordan? What was my identity as a Jordan? As you can see, I embraced it and now the name Jordan represents me and my children. We own this name. I was given this name because I married Jay, but I possess this name because of me.

I never realized how dependent I had become on his affections and flattery. My self-esteem took a huge blow.

I wasn't being called beautiful every day. I wasn't being doted on. My motherhood wasn't being complimented every day. I wasn't told how much he loved me every day. Maybe for some people that isn't a big deal, and I wouldn't have thought it would be for me either, till it was gone in a blink of an eye. Then it was like the wind in my self-esteem sails had just ceased. Stopped. No warning. I was dead in the water of life without the wind to move me.

I am a romantic, so romance and doting are a part of what makes me tick. Jay was a wonderful student of me. He was willing to learn all my little idiosyncrasies, and I was acclimated to that environment. Don't get me wrong, he didn't kiss my butt or worship me in any way. He was willing to tell me all about myself and what a jerk I could be. Because we were one, he appreciated being able to love me. To Jay, there was absolutely no one else on this planet for him but me, and if you ask anyone who knew us, they would tell you the same thing. I would walk out of the bathroom dressed for work, and he would be there doting. I would get out of the car after working all day, and he would be there doting. It was so hard to lose that. We didn't end up with five kids because we wanted kids. They just kept showing up to the party! I told Jay by the time I was pregnant with baby five that I wasn't going to wash our pants in the same laundry load anymore because this wasn't working out for me. We clearly were one, and had four solid representations of that fact.

I had to learn how to be a widowed, single mom of five people. I didn't birth five people by myself, yet here I was, alone with five kids. I struggled with resentments and hated it. I absolutely hated being a widowed mom. I kept asking, "Where is Jay?!" It felt like such a betrayal that he was gone. I didn't understand why it was then, with so many kids at such young ages, that I had to do all this alone. I would look at them and see him. For a little while, it was a stab to my heart. Now it is so endearing as I see traits in them that they got from their dad. Maybe endearing isn't always the word I would use, but for the most part it is. I just remind God regularly that pay back for teenage years dies with the person. I was a wife and mother; then I was just a mother. Where was Jay?

A great gift God gave me, definitely a beauty in the ashes of this widowed mom journey, was the release of feeling so responsible for my children. I am only one person that can be in one place doing one thing at one time. That doesn't bode well for having five children. So God taught me to release my children to Him and trust Him with them. Rest in that He is omniscient and omnipresent and able to cover them became my consistent mindset of parenting. Two people have a hard time keeping up with five children, but for one person, it is impossible. I learned that God would fill in the gaping cracks of my parent role, I just had to let go and let Him.

The art of becoming un-one is what every widow and widower will face. Who they are without their person will be a journey itself. How they are going to operate and move forward is a separate one. I would describe it this way: if you divorce, it is like two stickers being ripped apart. You will have pieces of you that go with the other person and pieces of them will stay with you. But when someone dies, your covenant is fulfilled. You are not leaving any of you behind. It is like two stickers having to slide apart. It is a slow and delicate movement. Each sticker is still whole, but one will be gone and the other will find another sticker.

My covenant with Jay was complete. God says that he promises to bring his work to completion, and I had to trust that Jay was complete on this side of heaven. We honored our covenant till the last breath. "Till death do us part," are the words we said that June day of 2004. We parted, and I was left here to carry on the work we had started together. It is an honor to raise these amazing kids. It is an honor to have had the chance to know Jay Jordan and to have been his person. Once the art of becoming un-one was complete, I felt whole in who I was.

Chapter 10

WHAT DID I LEARN ABOUT LIFE?

GRATEFULNESS IS A LIFEGIVER

Life is one of the most beautiful gifts that God has ever given us. I am grateful each day that I wake up and have another day, knowing how fast it can slip away. Every new day has challenges and things to overcome, but it also has so many blessings and things to celebrate. I celebrate that I can stand and walk. I celebrate that I have amazing kids. I celebrate that I am breathing. I watched Jay turn blue and his breath be taken. I will always be thankful that I have breath in my lungs.

Being grateful is probably one of the hardest things to do when death has entered your life. Death is so violating. However, gratefulness is humbling. When I wanted to die, the days I really struggled with suicidal thoughts because I hated everything, I would have to dig really deep inside and allow God to minister to my broken heart. In addiction recovery, they call it "playing out the tape." I would have to play out the tape of the thinking I was spiraling into. I would think about my kids. They were the gifts God had given me, and they cared, they would miss me, and they wanted me here. I became so incredibly grateful for my kids. I don't even know if they know what a saving grace they all were for me, but I tell them all the time how grateful I am for them.

I learned to be grateful for big things and little things. Sometimes it was the smallest things. A smile from someone. A kind word. Someone wanting to come visit. I began to look at things through a very different life lens. It was a gift of experiencing that level of loss.

LOVE HARD AND FORGIVE

Love hard and forgive. This became my life tagline. I mean it today as much as I did then. So I am going to say to you, my reader, what I encourage and challenge all my friends to do. You will never regret being kind to your loved ones. You will never regret saying a million "I love yous." You will never regret the nice things and the kind things. You will never regret saying you're sorry for being mean. You will never regret forgiving the petty things we all tend to get stuck on in relationships. You will always find peace in the place of grace with your loved ones.

You will regret not loving hard. You will wish that you had said one more "I love you" or given that last kiss. You will wish you had told them more and loved harder. You will wish that you had let that annoying thing go. You will regret all the words never said and all the beauty you withheld. So today, reading this, change it all! Love hard. Forgive!

I would tell my married friends to go make out with their husbands because they could. I would tell them to put the phone down and go have sex right now because they could. You don't realize how much you will miss sex until your person dies. It is awful! That was something I had never considered before but you will miss sex so much. So go have some! If your spouse is still here, put this book down and go have sex. Especially if it's been a while, go enjoy your person and allow the beauty of the gift of sex with your spouse to be enjoyed.

There is only one relationship that you are able to have sex, so enjoy it as much as possible. You will never regret having that moment with your spouse. It is such a beautiful gift of oneness that you don't experience with anyone else. Forgive your spouse for not being perfect because none of us are. We hold onto so many little petty things because we don't know how to let them pale in comparison to something as large as death. That last thing he/she did to piss you off is nothing in light of your entire life being tsunamied. It just isn't. I am not saying that you shouldn't acknowledge issues, I am saying don't get stuck on pettiness. You will never regret loving hard and forgiving.

CONQUER LIFE TO THE FULL

I began to live bigger than I had in the past. I am more willing to gauge things differently. For example, Jay would always take the kids to Dollar General and buy them stupid little things that probably were in the trash by the end of the day. I used to give him such a hard time because I told him that he was teaching the kids poor money management and that it was fiscally irresponsible. Those things are true, but after he died, I realized that maybe the memories the kids had of him spending that time with them was more important.

Because I am me, I couldn't do that exact thing. I still stand that it teaches poor money management. However, I began to weigh things my kids might want, or want to do, on a different scale. Is this memory making, even if it is expensive or not, the best idea? If it was going to make a memory, something they would cherish, it became worth it.

I started making bigger deals out of small things because I knew that there was no guarantee that we could ever do it again. I started appreciating the small moments and learned how to be more present. Instead of always looking to the next thing that would be happening, I began to be able to sit and soak up the moments. If we were on vacation somewhere, I would sit back and watch the kids and thank God for this moment. I would take the time to search for seashells or build a drip sand castle. I really wanted to absorb life in a new way.

I took the trip to see my brother defend his thesis in California. I went to see my nephew graduate in Colorado. I visited friends. As the years have passed, I haven't lost the desire to live life to the fullest. I realize that tomorrow isn't promised, and today is all I have.

ALL BY MY SELFIE

This became a hashtag that I would use when I would post a selfie. After Jay passed, and I was looking for pictures for his memorial service, I realized how many pictures I had of him and the kids with him, but not of us or me or all of us. So now, I take a selfie so fast! I will take selfies anytime and gather people in them. I find them to be really fun. I want to capture moments and life. I want my kids to have plenty of pictures of me and of all of us together. People who have not experienced a close loss, yet, often do not understand the importance of a picture.

When a picture is all that you have left, they are super valuable. When you know that there will come a moment that you will never be able to capture the likeness of that person again, it inspires you to conquer the moment. The Cure (the best band of all time) has a song called *Pictures of You*, and I think about that song when I am forgetful to capture times spent with people I love

Take the pictures. Take the selfies.

I also learned to do all sorts of things alone. I can go to movies, shows, concerts, and just about anywhere alone and not feel awkward. At first, it felt awkward to not have someone with me. Jay and I had done everything together for over eleven years by the time he passed away. I felt small and conspicuous. Like I had an invisible sign attached to my forehead with a large "W" on it, announcing to everyone that I am a widow and broken.

Truly, I was just being self-conscious. No one else cared that I was by myself. So go do the thing that you want to do. Live until you die, but never let death hold you captive from living.

We only have one life. Whether you are alone or coupled, the journey can still be amazing. I would rather be by myself, and know that I continued to live a full journey, than allow something that happened to me to steal the rest of what I have been given. Death is a thief, but you decide how much it steals sans your loved one.

DON'T GET STUCK
IN THEIR LOVE

Jay was the standard by which I knew love for over a decade. His love was my love. I didn't know that I had gotten stuck in his love. I didn't know that I measured everyone to Jay's love because it was what I knew. It seemed like it was what love was, except it isn't.

Trying to work out a new romantic relationship that was in a hard place, a sweet, dear friend of mine said to me, "You have to let Jay's love go. Those are too big of shoes to fill. No one is going to love you just like he did." I proceeded to burst into tears. That might have been some of the rawest, most needed truthfulness anyone has ever said to me. I couldn't accept this man's love on his terms because I was measuring it, even unknowingly, against Jay's love for me. I was robbing him of loving me in his way because I couldn't let myself move, pivot, or shift into a new love. Once again, my mind was blown! I had never realized that I was holding this new love, for me, captive.

I began to really look at myself and give myself room to change. I needed to let Jay go more, again. I needed to let his love be what was and not what is. I needed to allow this new love to be my standard of love because he was my now. This love is my present.

This man had a lot of patience at times dealing with my widowhood journey. I can't imagine what it is like to have to share heart space with someone else. He had moments of jealousy that we have had to walk through. He had to accept that Jay, a man he's never met and doesn't know, is always a part of our family. Once my dear friend spoke the truth that brought healing, I believe that this love was able to enjoy me more because I accepted his love. I am not in comparison land anymore. Truly, I had to release my love I lost. It is harder with widowhood because there aren't any of the negative emotions, like anger, hate, or resentment, that cause the desire to want a change. Change was forced upon me, and that is harder to shift when that love is gone.

If you have lost a spouse, learning to let go of their love will be so hard but so worth it. You, like me, will have to release any love you have lost. Keep working through your grief. I am going to give you the same words that my wise friend gave me: those shoes are too big to fill, you have to let go of that love.

It is easy to idolize someone who is dead. It is easy to forget how aggravating they could be. Death seems to remove any importance of taking your stand on any point. Sometimes we become trapped in their love because we fail to remember the fullness of the person, and that they weren't perfect. Even wonderful relationships have trials, so remembering that there were good and bad times, just like the new person in your life brings, will help you accept their love. You may choose not to have a new love, and that is OK.

Sometimes Friends Show Up in Unexpected Places

I met new people that I would have never met had it not been for this journey. I met other fellow widows, some who were further down the journey than I was, and they would encourage me. Some were new widows who, as time passed for me, I could encourage. I would message them to check in on them. I know the crazy that comes along with the widow brain, so I always try to encourage them to dig into those feelings and be honest. It is a scary place to be and feels vulnerable, but because I could understand, I would push a little harder to get past the "I'm OK," or "I'm doing fine," generic responses. Sometimes I would back off and just let them share what was on their minds but not push for them to walk a little further. The grief journey is delicate and difficult. I don't know that I can even equate it with anything.

You have to be incredibly strong and resilient to make the journey, yet so incredibly vulnerable and weak. It truly is a precious place to have a friend. My widow friends were a critical part of my journey. I am so grateful for them to this day, and though many are no longer living as widows, I love seeing their new lives blossoming. The trials of being a remarried widow is unique as well, so I believe being able to continuously have support from people who "get it" is nice.

There were some really awesome people who never shied away from us during this complex journey. I don't know that I can ever express the gratitude that I have for them. Pressing in toward a difficult time in someone's life is a beautiful show of deep character.

There were some people who were encouraged by me as I walked a difficult path. I have had people reach out to me through messages because they wanted my advice or input on what would be the best way to handle a difficult place that they were in. That was maybe one of the most humbling parts of this journey that I never considered. Someone may be watching me survive, so they survived too. I hope I encouraged them well, because trauma is a hard path to walk.

Chapter 11

JESUS, THE WELL WOMAN, AND ME

There is a story in the Bible about the woman at a well. Jesus is with his disciples and sends them on their way to run an errand, and he waited at the well for this Samaritan woman. Why did he wait for her? I have heard this story taught from pulpits many times, and it never made sense to me. Until I became a widow.

The Samaritan woman was at the well in the middle of the day, which was unusual. It would have been very hot, and she would have been vulnerable to anyone around her that may potentially harm her. I think this woman became one of *those* women. The vulnerable ones and the ones without a place anymore. The widow. The passage tells us that she was living with a man who wasn't her husband but had had five husbands. When I hear this taught from others, they say this woman was divorced. I believe this woman was a widow, potentially with many losses. With each loss her heart hardened a little more. With each loss she felt a little closer to Death than to Life. By the time she got to the relationship she was in, what was even the point in getting married when he was probably just going to die on her?

See, her life had been tsunamied enough times that she no longer cared about "normal" functioning around others. Nothing was normal about her world. She didn't want to go to the well and hear all the other women hen-pecking about their husbands and their families. She didn't want to hear about the lady's husband who fixed the fence and helped with the kids. Brutal reminders of how Death had stolen all of that from her.

Then one day, unexpectedly, she has a divine date. God sees her. He knows what she needs. Jesus shows up in all his grace and mercy and asks her to draw him some water. She is confused about why this Jewish man would even talk to her, she is Samaritan after all, and a woman. But Jesus came to be the redeemer of all humans, so her status and gender and class were of no concern. Her heart, however, mattered to Him more than anything. He tells this woman that if she would drink the water that he would give her, she would never have to be thirsty again. Confused, she says that she wasn't sure that that was possibly a real thing, to not be thirsty again.

He asked her to go get her husband, to which she replied that she didn't have a husband. He went straight to the place that death had touched her. He went to the sore spot first, husband. He told her that she was right; she had had five husbands, and the man she was living with wasn't her husband. She admitted that he must be a prophet to know this information about her without her telling him. She didn't know she was talking to God Himself. But why would God care about this woman, who had faced more death than imaginable, who had forgotten all about life? Because God's very purpose of sending Jesus was to defeat death and restore life.

The living water is what Jesus calls the water He is going to give her parched, dry, and destitute heart. Living. Jesus focused on what she needed, which was the purpose of Him coming to Earth. Life! She needed living water to erase the damage death had created. Once she accepted Jesus' living water, everything changed. She had life again. Jesus' specialty is bringing life out of death.

When God first gave me the revelation about the woman at the well, I was in awe. I always wondered why Jesus didn't chastise her about her sin, living with a man she wasn't married to. See, the adulterous woman, who was about to be stoned, Jesus addressed her sin. So why not with this woman? I believe it is because Jesus knew that a tsunamied life, which has had the Great Nothing come in and take everything, needs LIFE FIRST!! It needs to be healed and whole and then we can approach the other issues. This woman needed to be able to breathe again. She needed to have hope again. She needed to have life.

I needed the same thing. I needed my dawn to crest from the long, hard night. I needed a renewal of hope and energy. Through this revelation of scripture, God gave me hope that He knew I needed life and that He is the Living Water. He surely restored my soul and my life in so many ways, but especially from death.

Chapter 12

LIVING LIFE TO THE FULL

One of the beautiful parts of being a widow is realizing how short life can be and how quickly and swiftly it can be taken. So I decided that I will forever live my life to the fullest. I will seize opportunities and not be afraid of tackling anything.

One of my fun hobbies is riding my Harley Davidson Sporster 48. I learned to ride my own motorcycle in the summer of 2019. Riding is therapeutic for me in many ways, but one in particular is that it forced me to be in the moment. That was such a contrast to my over-planning brain that it was like a brain rest. I wasn't really much of a super planner before widowhood. I preferred to handle most things flying by the seat of my pants, but widowhood, with its incredibly hard and constant demands forced me to become a planner. To keep the train moving, I planned nearly everything six months in advance. Riding forced me to be in the moment. I had to look at the road, traffic, stay upright, and lean through my curves. Each moment was taken up with something imminent that could cause harm. I still love to get on my motorcycle and take long rides, especially when my brain needs a rest from over thinking.

I will never sit down and pretend that every second I have breath isn't a gift from God. I will do what I know Jesus came for, to give us life abundantly. I love to conquer each day, though I am definitely not always in a good mood. I teach my children to live life to the fullest as well. They love to take on new challenges, taste new foods, and try new things. We enjoy getting to do this together. I often share with them how adventurous Jay was and how much he loved to live life. We have hilarious conversations about how ridiculous he could be and how obtuse some things he did were. There was one night we were at a restaurant when he was holding Rebekah, who was probably fifteen months old at the time, and she was back washing her food into a glass of water that Jay was letting her drink. Right before we left, he picked up the cup of water and started drinking it. When he put it down, he saw all the floaties of food in it, and we were all like, "EEEWWW!!" It was disgusting, but he didn't realize it had all that yuck in it til he had taken a big swallow. Now we laugh as we tell that story.

I value memory making more than anything. If I go anytime soon, I want my kids to have a ton of memories to pull from to make them smile. Especially on the hard days, when life seems overwhelming and maybe not worth it, knowing that life is a gift helps me to press on. I hope that I instill that in them too.

Finding joy in the little and mundane things has become a pursuit of mine. I tend to overlook life trying to keep everything going and together, but in the last few years, God has begun to teach me to look at each day with more joy and more appreciation. He will remind me to look at how beautiful my yard is or how pretty the sunset is. There is a Japanese maple that lives across the street from me that brings me much pleasure! Sometimes I will be driving home and just thank God for the views on the way. The sunsets with their beautiful colors that set the sky on fire and a blaze in my heart, or maybe the colors are pastel like cotton candy and it makes me feel soft and childlike. I get to drive past Sloss Furnace, the place that Jay and I got married, and overlook the cityscape and it captures my heart everytime. I realize that life is made of the small things, the mundane things, and the easily overlooked things, like the moments of laughter from an overheard conversation. We focus so much on the big things and big events, that we miss the beauty of the life lived in the middle. Death taught me that life is so important and beautiful!

If I hope to honor Jay's legacy with anything, it is to love Jesus. Jay's redemption story in Christ is one of the most amazing parts of his whole story. He loved Jesus more than anything, and he never forgot where he came from. Jesus came that we would have life and have it to the full (John 10:10). He made a specific trip to the woman at the well, then He went to the cross for you and I. If you have faced Death, and it stole someone you love, the best thing you can do is live!

Chapter 13

GOD, GUM, GRIT, AND GRACE

God, gum, grit, and grace. These are the primary components to survival. Boundaries cannot be overlooked because they were critical, but they don't start with a "g," so I left them out of my alliteration sentence.

I am humbled by how God walked each and every step with me through the Valley of the Shadow of Death. He helped me pick up my tsunamied life piece by piece and rebuild it. He was patient, kind, and even pushy at times. Building my relationship with God for the decade before I ended up here was critical. I knew the character and commitment of God when my world went into the tailspin, and I never, for one second, thought I was alone walking through that dark valley. The pinprick of Light was steady and constant. I could see because of it and had hope for the future.

There were plenty of times that I saturated myself in the, "Why me?" and, "Where is God in this?" questions. Sometimes it was hard to see any answers when my disappointment was overwhelming. I was disappointed that

I was left to do all this alone. I was also disappointed in the Church and her lack of caring and consideration, despite God specifically calling believers to take care of widows and orphans. I had to fight hard and rest in Jesus not to allow bitterness to rear its ugly head. But God. God always showed up and allowed me to be in the moment of pain, but He never left me there. He always loved me to a place of healing and forgiveness. I had to remind myself that no one really knew what I needed, including me.

I don't think that dissolves the responsibility of the local churches to show up and help widows and orphans. I hope to help with that on a large scale someday by creating a structured, practical way of teaching churches how to help widows long term. God will make a way when the time is right, and it will be another healing step for me. God's patience and love has been so consistent, beautiful, and unwavering that I am humbled by it and hope to pass it along to others.

Gum. I probably should have taken stock out in a gum company. I chewed gum constantly to work through my stress and anxiety. Napping and gum. Those were my constant coping mechanisms and allowed my mind to rest and my body to process. My body took a serious blow from the trauma. My endocrine system blew out. I was diagnosed with hypothyroidism. Then my adrenal system blew out because I was living on adrenalin to function on the constant insanely busy days. I thought that I was developing fibromyalgia because my joints would hurt. It was random and on different days it was different parts. One day my shoulder, one day my knee, it never had a pattern. I was falling apart physically. Grief was taking its toll on my physical body. Gum was a helpful way to process for me. I would chew on that gum like a cow eats cud. Then I would replace that utterly destroyed piece with a new piece and continue to filter my feelings through my jaws.

In 2019, I knew I was extremely sick on my inside. I was swelling out of clothes that I had purchased within the month that I bought them. I thought I was going to have to get surgery to open my eyelids again because my eyes were so small. I would be doubled over in pain by the end of a work day, and I couldn't handle wearing jeans anymore because of the pressure they put on my abdomen. I had so much pain in my body. My diet didn't help. It's hard when your heart has nowhere to land but into a dang bag of chips. I also ate whatever I wanted, like my body hadn't just been put through hell. I was fairly ignorant about health, and I couldn't understand what was happening to me. I had a friend that sent me to a naturopath, and it has changed my entire understanding of the body and health. I have pursued natural and genuine health for the last four years. I have recovered from so much damage internally and continue to get better every day. My eyes are opened normally again. My joints no longer hurt. My body has been able to filter and process so much. I am gluten free now because gluten was killing me, but I would have never known that if I hadn't taken the steps to get well. This part of healing took as much grit as any other part of my grief journey.

Grit is the moxie that kept me alive. I refused to give up on myself, my children, and life as whole. I was gonna army crawl myself through that dark valley if I had to. Like a battle-wounded warrior, I was going to bleed my emotions, and take every broken heart with every residual goodbye, and rebuild my life. The residual goodbyes were one thing I never expected. Shutting his cell phone off. Cleaning his clothes out. Packing away things that were his. Painting over his fingerprints. All residual goodbyes, including this book. This book is another goodbye to so much I've held inside for so many years. Another step away from widowhood and another building block to rebuilding my life. Rebuilding a tsunamied life requires grit. There is no other way to do it. I am grateful that my natural personality has a lot of grit and moxie. My brother calls me indomitable. I intend to get that tattooed on me one day. All these words: grit, moxie, and indomitable are my battle cries. I embrace them with wholeheartedness. They represent me to my core. Without them, I truly don't know that I would have survived this season.

Grace may be one of my favorite things on this planet. I, for the first time in my life, had grace for everyone. People say the dumbest things when you are in grief. They want to encourage you or support you, but what they really do is make you want to punch them in the mouth. Anytime I see someone has experienced loss, the only thing I type these days is "loss sucks." That is all I really wanted to hear. Not sorry... I never could figure out what that meant. I thought,"You didn't do anything. Are you feeling sorry for me? How are you sorry? Why are you sorry?" It didn't make any sense to me. I recognize it comes from a place of not knowing what to say, and it seems compassionate, but it truly annoyed me. "God wouldn't give you this if you couldn't handle it," might be one of the most ignorant and stupid things that someone can say. Again, I know that the heart was meant to encourage me, but I really just wanted to offer to exchange places with them and let God work on their strength. I was all out.

I had to learn the beauty of grace and what it meant for me and everyone around me. I would often make posts on social media that would say, "Grace to everyone for being asshats." Because we all have our moments of being asshats and say and do dumb things. We need to practice grace for each other. Allow others to be stupid sometimes. Allow others to make mistakes and be able to say sorry. Allow others to be a human mess in need of a Savior named Jesus and just saturate it all in His grace. I offer more grace now than I have at any other time in my life. My indomitable moxie has to be tempered by grace. Without grace, grit can be viciously cold. I couldn't become cold and keep my children thriving. I had to remain malleable and soft and loving, even when I was fighting against it.

There were times that I longed to shell up in bitterness and anger and allow it to protect me. It seemed safer there sometimes. But there is no life in that place, and life was what I intended on living, so I had to keep myself saturated in grace. God, gum, grit, and grace marked the years of widowhood, like a Swiss army knife, a multi-tool of survival.

CONCLUSION

I hope that if you are walking the widowhood journey, that you can take nuggets out of my journey and apply it to your walk. Hang in there! Keep going! There is so much beautiful life to be lived. I am proud of you for making it this far! Each step you take, each breath you take, are huge wins!

There is no greater nightmare, other than the loss of a child, when you get married than losing your partner, lover, best friend, confidant, and the father/mother of your kids. Every single married person thinks about what it may be like, or they avoid ever letting that thought cross their mind out of fear, but there is no way to avoid that thinking about losing our love leaves chills down our spines. The only relationship in our lives with which we become one flesh is with our spouse, who we are meant to spend every day with, hopefully growing old, until death separates us. So, if you have found yourself in that nightmare, and you look around and your life has been tsunamied by Death, you will possibly struggle with feeling like there is no reason to go on.

When Death summons your heart, and it seems like it would be easier to give in and give up, remind Death that he was defeated in the beautiful resurrection of Jesus. A defeated foe is always easier to fight against than one you feel like you have to war against yourself. Jesus met Death on his territory so He could take back that ground for us as victors. After the death of someone we have dedicated our lives to, sometimes living seems like the evil part. I promise you that life is the beautiful gift of surviving. Choose to live.

If you haven't experienced loss, I appreciate you spending time learning about my journey, and I hope that it helps you walk along with someone who may be hurting and lost in the dark valley. If their life has been tsunamied, they may not know how to ask for help, primarily because there is so much to be done, they don't even know where to begin. If you will just stay present, you will help make an impact and a difference. Show up. Don't quit. As the months go on, you will be needed just as much six months in, a year in, two years in, as you are in the beginning.

ENCOURAGEMENT STEPS FOR WIDOWS/WIDOWERS

1. Journal daily to free your mind of all the things you need to say
   a. You can use paper and pen
   b. Use your phone in the notes app
   c. Use your computer and make a document
      Write as often as you need to

2. Find healthy coping mechanisms to filter your emotions
   a. Napping
   b. Chewing gum
   c. Exercise
   d. Therapy
      Do not use drugs, alcohol, or food to cope

3. Get involved in a grief group
   a. This will help you have support with others that can relate to what you are going through
   b. You will be able to identify feelings that you may not otherwise be able to identify

4. Pay attention to your body
   a. Grief consists of emotions, mental, and body
   b. Your body may get sick from grief
      i. Eat well
      ii. Work with a naturopath/chiropractor to help you stay healthy
   c. Rest as much as you need to
      i. This is a marathon healing, not a sprint.
      ii. Take as long as you need to heal. There is no right or wrong way or time for healing to take place.

5. Practice Grit and Grace
   a. Grit: this will not allow you to give up with you want to
   b. Grace: this will allow you to let the stupid and hard things roll off your back
      no need to carry more load than you already have on you!

ABOUT THE AUTHOR

Stephanie Jordan is an author, teacher, cosmetologist, salon owner, passionate Jesus follower, and mother to five amazing kids. Birmingham, AL is called home. Sharing her journey of God's faithfulness in the face of trials and teaching others the depth of God's love has become her life's work. She has been married, divorced and widowed.

When she is not writing or speaking, you can find her riding a Harley Davidson Sportster 48, flaunting new healthy gluten free recipes on her Facebook group; The Recovering Southerner, painting, reading, watching movies with the family, and spending time outdoors. She has launched a family reunion a.k.a. "Church" called The Garbage Can. The goal of The Garbage Can is to raze hell and build the kingdom of God by answering questions: who, what, when, where, why, and how for scripture.

Other titles by Stephanie:

Believing in Boundaries:
Using Biblical Teaching to Understand and Establish
Healthy Modern Boundaries

US link: https://www.amazon.com/dp/B0B1W6SQNK
UK link: https://www.amazon.co.uk/dp/B0B1W6SQNK
Canada link: https://www.amazon.ca/dp/B0B1W6SQNK

Follow her social media:

Instagram: https://www.instagram.com/thestephaniejordan/
@thestephaniejordan

Facebook: https://www.facebook.com/TheStephanieJordan

LinkedIn: The Stephanie Jordan

YouTube: https://www.youtube.com/@thestephaniejordan.
@thestephaniejordan.

TikTok: thestephaniejordan

CAN YOU HELP ME?

Thank you for reading my book!

I really appreciate all of your feedback, and I love
hearing what you have to say.
I need your input to make the next version of this
book and my future books better.

Please leave me an honest review on Amazon or the
store where you purchased the book, letting me know
how this book touched you and what I can do to
improve the content.

Made in the USA
Columbia, SC
13 November 2023

25908678R00083